SUICIDE

The Constructive/Destructive Self

SUICIDE

The Constructive/Destructive Self

Coletta A. Klug

Studies in Health and Human Services
Volume 25

The Edwin Mellen Press
Lewiston/Queenston/Lampeter

Library of Congress Cataloging-in-Publication Data

Klug, Coletta A.
    Suicide : the constructive/destructive self / Coletta A. Klug.
        p.   cm. -- (Studies in health and human services ; v. 25)
    Includes bibliographical references and index.
    ISBN 0-7734-8830-8 (hard)
    1. Youth--Suicidal behavior. 2. Youth--Mental health.
3. Adaptation (Psychology) 4. Suicide--Prevention. I. Title.
II. Series.
RJ506.S9K58 1996
362.2'8'0835--dc20   96-4678
                                              CIP

This is volume 25 in the continuing series
Studies in Health and Human Services
Volume 25 ISBN 0-7734-8830-8
SHHS Series ISBN 0-88946-126-0

A CIP catalog record for this book is available from the British Library.

The Edwin Mellen Press   The Edwin Mellen Press
Box 450   Box 67
Lewiston, New York   Queenston, Ontario
USA 14092-0450   CANADA L0S 1L0

The Edwin Mellen Press, Ltd.
Lampeter, Dyfed, Wales
UNITED KINGDOM SA48 7DY

Printed in the United States of America

DEDICATION

To My Sister, Bernie, RN
who inspired and encouraged
My Nursing Career

and

To *All* My Students
Through the Years

TABLE OF CONTENTS

PREFACE

In the initial orientation to Nursing, in my training program, I learned about mental health and mental illness but the programs in that era of time provided for didactic content with little or no opportunity to work with clients in a psychiatric setting. In a few short years after graduation — working with beginning nursing students in clinical practice and experience with veterans in Veterans' Hospitals, it was clear to me that there was a need for experience in Psychiatry.

My curiosity was aroused to later choose a two-year experience in a 2000 bed Veteran's Hospital, solely for patients who carried a psychiatric diagnosis, and later was assigned to a unit of Psychiatry as part of a Medical-Surgical care. My experience with these patients in the role of Staff Nurse, Acting Head Nurse and Head Nurse provided me with insight and a personal commitment to pursue my Baccalaureate study followed by a Master's degree in Psychiatric Nursing. My foundation course interests strongly focused on Psychology and Sociology and this knowledge led me down the Graduate path to Psychiatric Nursing. Graduate Study in Education, in Curriculum Development, came later at The State University of New York at Buffalo.

In my clinical experience I have worked with many clients who were suicidal or had bouts of suicidal ideation, followed through with threats to unresolved problems, and occasionally suicidal attempts. There was the unfortunate periodic experience of having a former client complete the suicidal act. This created a feeling of loss and a sensation of failure that affected all members of the mental health team formerly involved. Actually, that feeling is almost impossible to describe.

I have been grateful to the former National Institute of Mental Health for some financial support at the graduate level, along with the psychological support of my professional associates, Doctors, Maurice Levine, S. Mouchly Small, Robert Daniels,

Robert Mockbee and Nurses, Bernadine C. Klug, Myrle P. King, Donna Juenker, Corinne Stuart, Marlene Werner, Florence Hennessey, Anne Sengbusch, Ruth McGrorey, Bonnie Bullough and Mecca Cranley.

In early clinical experience, the actual intervention with patients who were undoubtedly suicidal was learned from colleagues and associates with years of experience, and the treatment of choice at that given time was not necessarily based on scientific research. Appropriate dialogue seemed quite incomplete with patients who were self-destructive, or had a destructive tendency which led me toward my research in `Attitudes of Physicians and Nurses Toward the Suicidal Patient,' as my Master's Thesis at Ohio State University, School of Nursing, Columbus, Ohio.

As a faculty member at The State University of New York at Buffalo, School of Nursing, Department of Psychiatric Nursing, it was a privilege to continue my research and study of suicide in becoming a member of Dr. Harvey Resnik's Study in Suicidology at The National Institute of Mental Health (1969-1970). This course focused on curriculum development of suicide assessment and intervention content in all the Humanities' Programs, carried out in teams of two University Schools for each discipline, about forty in all. At the completion of this special program, participants were expected to return to their respective schools and initiate an educational program, developing content of suicidology in the School Curriculum, if possible. At that time, content directed toward care of the suicidal patient was conspicuous by its absence, for example, a text in any one of the health-care disciplines might have only one chapter devoted to the topic of suicide, in a fairly general context.

Originally, the course accepted by the SUNYAB — School of Nursing Curriculum Committee was a two-credit Elective course, initially taught to a group of twenty-five senior Nursing students. After more than a ten-year period this elective course was made available to non-nurses and finally it had few or no prerequisites to enroll in the course. Concepts of Wellness and Holistic Health became more popular, and in 1984, the Course was changed to a three-credit elective, `The Constructive/Destructive Self,' enveloping the holistic concept of health from my graduate work, which emphasized lifestyle as one of the major factors leading to self-destructive behavior.

The breadth of the course requires a text to encompass the Holistic Wellness Concept, using the Travis Wellness Inventory, to the destructive lifestyles that frequently result in suicide. It is anticipated that students will have completed a course in Human Growth and Development, or are currently registered while completing this elective course.

This initial chapter focusing on suicide serves as a baseline for the course. Although most students approach the course with a fair knowledge of normal nutrition, the course makes theoretical nutritional reference through a professional videotape. This course moves progressively from a healthy growth and development review and a constructive lifestyle toward some destructive lifestyles with the latter part of the course focusing on the problem of suicide in our society at all ages, including elderly, but with major emphasis on adolescence and young adults. Attention is directed to destructive lifestyle patterns that apparently contribute to suicidal behavior. Every effort is made to convince students that suicide is not an answer to our society's psychosocial dilemma, but is utilized all too often by young adults and others as the solution to their unsolved problems.

It is my contention that Lifestyle doesn't just happen — it is chosen, and most youth can be assisted and directed toward constructive behavior that leads them to a healthy lifestyle rather than a destructive pattern which frequently ends in suicide.

In my textbook, every effort has been made to encompass course content by beginning with the problem of suicide, followed by an obvious constructive lifestyle base to precede the possible destructive pattern that has a potential to lead the individual to suicide. Intervention techniques are unique with a strong preventive dimension, through improving basic communication skills, use of music, dance, humor, pets, and a general direction toward creative expression.

Coletta A. Klug, Ed.D., RN.
State University of New York at Buffalo
School of Nursing
Associate Professor, Emeritus

INTRODUCTION

In Part I, initially, the problem of self-destructive behavior by suicide is addressed as a psychosocial problem that warrants alarm, especially for the younger generation.

Theorists who have attempted to provide a better understanding of this problem, as Freud, Durkheim, Henry and Short, Schneidman and Farberow, Haim, Litman, Lester, and others are included, who are continuing to make valuable contributions to society regarding this topic.

The assessment and evaluation of potential suicides are touched upon with some suggestions as to how to prevent and/or intervene proficiently.

The complexity of this proposition is obvious with statistics indicating that suicides are increasing progressively during the past quarter century. Dealing with the realities of the self early in the life of a child seems to be the best indication for prevention of problems at this time.

Part II describes the normal human development followed by the life processes — learning about the self and how to relate to others in day-to-day living, with family and later with others outside the family. It is strongly inferred that the strong, healthy family is the basic support for an individual who hopefully will find him/herself in a school with a nurturing environment at all levels, and especially in early childhood experiences. Normal stress that all humans are subject to at some level is explained as normal to a degree, but that also depends upon the individual's strength and attitude toward life and its meaning.

Some phases of life develop into crisis situations, when intervention and adaptation need to be addressed by the individual. If crises are successfully dealt with in younger life, the individual has an opportunity to learn how to deal with crisis in later years.

Loss is universally experienced, generally speaking. Although grief is an experience for almost everyone who lives on, there are many variables that affect an individual's grieving process. Cultural beliefs and what an individual is exposed to early in the family will affect the adaptation process of most human beings.

Part III provides examples of destructive human behavior related to Addictions — Alcohol and Other Drugs.

In dealing with depression it is not entirely clear how much control an individual has over the resolution from depression, considering there are various levels of depression and that not all people are handicapped by this mood disorder.

The Abusive Family has become definitely problematic in our affluent society. This topic recognizes recent research findings, and a model of the abusive family is proposed by Stanton (1993).

Part IV relates examples generally of constructive behavior. Content begins with contributions from students' classroom experiences. Primarily these were written by students but some were samples of conceptual fingerpainting, added as a personal learning tool and technique.

Creative Arts include Rhythm, Music and Dancing and describe significance in each of our lives.

Pets are considered as positive possessions for prevention to psychosocial problems in most peoples' lives. They can also be uniquely used as tools of intervention for many people of all ages, when they are ill.

Humor has been used as an adjunct therapy and is finding its place in the literature during the past decade as a regular treatment. Norman Cousins personally utilized humor from films for his own health problem he described as quite successful, and perhaps was one of the interventions that extended his life a number of years.

From the reader's point of view, they are brought to the reality of death through the self-destructive means of suicide, and by means of society's view of life and death by Euthanasia. It is now a timely topic from everyone's point of view, and eventually it may well be related to an economic dilemma. Hence, the question, 'What Does the Future Hold?'

PART I

INTRODUCTION

CHAPTER I

Suicide The Problem

Suicide -- the taking of one's life -- is a complex behavioral phenomenon influenced by a wide range of social and biological factors. It would seem that suicide is a phenomenon copyrighted by man. To our knowledge, the animal does not commit suicide, apparently because it has neither consciousness nor a conception of death. Failure to comprehend or accept finality of death is an important feature of suicide in the young, the aged, and among certain primitive peoples who do not perceive the suicide act as essentially one of self-destruction. Although suicide has been sanctioned by many in our society over the past few years, there is continued controversy as to whether we as individuals have the right to take our own lives, but most cultures regard suicide as irrational.

Young and old seem to have much in common regarding suicide. They rarely see their act as terminal and ending in death, but rather as a process. It may be inflicting guilt or causing pain to significant persons, central to, or responsible for the loss they have sustained. The process may be directed toward eliciting love and affection, or it can be one by which the suicidal person seeks to be reborn or reunited with a lost, loved one. There may be any number of influences that can help to generate suicidal behavior. In this text, we shall attempt to discuss some of the influences, direct or indirect, which appear relevant to this author.

It is necessary to consider the total personality with its strivings and conflicts as a basis for suicide. Human behavior is determined to a large extent by interaction of heredity, early life experiences, and environmental factors. Some believe the primary cause of suicide stems from childhood, perhaps during an earlier developmental stage when the child felt rejected by the parents. If the rejected feeling is not overcome, so they suggest, by a sustained feeling of acceptance by one or more human beings, the individual may react to adverse circumstances by a suicidal act at some time later in life. This chapter will focus particularly on youth, adolescents and young adults.

Haim (1970) went into detail as to physical and psychological changes during adolescence. From a social point of view, she described adolescence as the period during which the individual gradually abandons infantile attitudes to other group members and attains a perception and acceptance of reality. This transition enables him/her to be admitted into the group on equal footing with others, realizing there are chronological limitations in some instances. Haim explained that suicide is not only a problem today, but it has been problematic for our Western culture going back at least to the beginning of the 20th century. From an ancient tradition, altruistic suicide — a person giving up his or her life for others for a greater good — has existed ever since humans have become clans. There are some reported current remnants of the urge toward altruistic suicide in sacrifices made by soldiers on the battlefield. For an earlier

---

Collected Papers, Vol. v by Sigmund Freud. [ed.] James Strachey (1952). Published by Basic Books, Inc. (a division of Harper Collins Publishers, Inc.) by arrangement of the *Hogarth Press, Ltd.* and *Institute of Psycho-Analysis.* London.

enlightenment of this topic, students may need to read or re-read the Old Testament for biblical accounts of four noted suicides, i.e., Samson, King Saul, Saul's servant and armor bearer, and Achitophel. The famous suicide in the New Testament is that of Judas Iscariot, after his betrayal of Jesus of Nazareth. Suicide has been studied, interpreted and reflected upon for centuries preceding our current reference, with controversy to extreme degrees as to the morality, legality, and acceptance of the act. According to Stillion et al (1989), the year of 1651 is the time line when the word *suicide* was introduced into the English language. In the middle of the 17th century, John Donne (1982) described the church teaching about suicide that had become rigid and suicide was considered sinful in the worst degree. Donne is credited with being the first to suggest that human beings have a natural desire to die as well as a desire to live.

Early Theories

Some basic theory from Sigmund Freud, interpreted by James Strachey (1952), it was noted that generally psycho-analysis endeavors to develop its theories as independently as possible from those theories of other sciences, however, it is obliged to seek a basis for the theory of instincts in biology. The set of instincts known well in analysis, the libidinal, sexual or life instincts, are best comprised under the name of *Eros* with their purpose to form living substance into even greater unities, so that life may be prolonged and brought to higher development. In the far-reaching consideration of processes which go to make up life and which lead to death, we should recognize the existence of two classes of instincts, corresponding to the contrary processes of construction and dissolution in the organism. The one set of instincts, working essentially in silence, would be those which follow the aim of leading the living creature to death and deserve to be called the *death instincts*, referred to as *Thanatos*.

4

These would be directed outwards as a result of the combination of numbers of unicellular elementary organisms, and would manifest themselves as *destructive* or *aggressive impulses*. Life would consist in the manifestations of the conflict or interaction between the two classes of instincts; death would mean the victory of the destructive instincts for the individual but reproduction would mean victory of Eros for him. This view would enable us to characterize instincts as tendencies inherent in living substance towards restoring an earlier state of things. Both classes of instincts in this view, Eros and Thanatos, would have been in operation and working against each other from the first origin of life.

Aetiology of suicide, Emile Durkheim (1951), was based on analysis of interconnectedness of suicide with social and natural phenomena with a wide variance. Durkheim has touched on normal and abnormal psychology, social psychology, anthropology, meteorology and other cosmic factors, such as religion, marriage, the family, divorce, primitive rites and customs, social and economic crises, crime and law, history, education, and occupational groups. He believed suicide could not be explained by its individual forms, and was a distinct phenomenon in its own right, as he related currents of suicide to social concomitants. Through his study of religious affiliation, marriage and the family, and political and national communities, Durkheim moved to the first of his three categories of suicide, *egoistic* suicide, resulting from lack of integration of the individual into society. Egoistic suicide was also seen where there was slight integration of the individual into the family life. Where the individual's life was rigorously governed by custom and habit, he called this *altruistic*

4

Emile Durkheim (1951). *Suicide a Study of Sociology* (J. Spaulding and G. Simpson, Trans.) New York: The Free Press (original work published 1897) (c) 1951, 1979 reprinted by permission of The Free Press a division of Simon and Schuster Inc.

suicide. This type of suicide he would find still existent in modern society where ancient patterns of obedience are common. The third form of suicide he called *anomic* suicide, which resulted from lack of regulation of the individual in society. The individual's needs and their satisfaction, according to this theory, have been regulated by society; the common beliefs and practices learned made the individual the embodiment of what Durkheim called collective conscience.

In the latter half of the 20th century many changes have occurred particularly related to an increase of medical discoveries and development of medical technology. Extension of the life expectancy approximately 30 years has resulted from increased knowledge of the disease process, knowledge and improvement of child-birth procedures, advances in prevention and treatment of disease generally, and for other reasons. In considering the prolongation of life by use of new electronic devices and the method of donor organs has led to the extensive cost, to age as a criterion and to ethical debates about the right to die. The similarities and differences between suicide and euthanasia are currently argued and will present serious considerations for future health care (Stillion et al., 1989).

The relationship of Suicide and Homicide was considered by Henry and Short (1954). These two acts were considered acts of aggression as they both react in the same way to the same objective frustrating source. The target is different since the self is the target in suicide while another person is the target of aggression in homicide. The conclusion was considered in part related to the strength of the external restraint over behavior. When behavior is required to conform rigidly to demands and expectations of other persons, the probability of suicide as a response to frustration is low while the probability of homicide is high. When behavior has less demand and requirement for conformity to others' expectations, the probability of suicide is high, while at the same time, probability of homicide is low. Consideration was given to legitimacy of aggression, that homicide would occur as a response to frustration only when the other-oriented expression of aggression was defined by the aggressor as highly legitimate, for example a declared war. Henry and Short (1954) explained: "'If it is true that war lowers the suicide rate and raises the homicide rate, holding constant the effect of business conditions, the explanation may lie in the fact that war not only legitimizes but acts to encourage the expression of aggression outwardly against the enemy. Frustration suffered during times of war can always be blamed on the enemy. The focusing of aggression against the opponent fulfills an important social function.'"

The strength of external restraints becomes primary basis for legitimization of other-oriented aggression. When behavior is required to conform rigidly to demands and expectations of others (when external restraints are strong), the proposition would suggest that the expression of aggression against others is legitimized. When behavior is subjected to strong external restraints in social relationships with other persons, the restraining objects can be blamed for frustrations and thereby legitimizing outward expression of the resultant aggression. When behavior is freed from external restraints the self must bear responsibility for frustration. Others cannot be blamed since others were not involved in determination of behavior. Under these conditions, other-oriented expressions of resultant aggression fails to legitimize. Assuming that the super ego means the system of demands and expectations imposed on the child by the parents as internalized by the child, this system of demands and

Andrew F. Henry and James F. Short (1954) *Suicide and Homicide.* New York: The Free Press. (c) (1954). Reprinted by permission of The Free Press, a division of Simon and Schuster, Inc.

expectations then becomes the system of demands and expectations imposed on the child himself. Ultimately the punitive super-ego operates to turn aggression against the self.

Early scholars, clerics, doctors and ordinary people have grappled with the question of why people kill themselves. So much in our tradition and culture motivates mankind toward living, but some people still try to end their lives. Theories attempting to explain reasons for this problem of suicide include blame to parents, blame to society, or blame to heredity or body chemistry, to name a few. One thing seems certain that no single cause can explain all suicides. In order even to attempt to unravel the mystery of suicide, which involves every aspect of life, one needs to consider society in which a person lives, to family background, to psychological makeup, and to childhood history.

ASSESSMENT AND EVALUATION

Suicide and Age

Generally, when persons between 20 and 39 years of age come to the attention of the therapist based on urges or attempts of suicide, one might expect to find more intense interpersonal motives operating in more than half of the patients; the chronic depressive feelings will probably be dominant in about one-fourth of the cases. Once the necessary medical measures have been taken, the method of treatment choice seems to be a type of dynamic psychotherapy, according to Shneidman and Farberow (1957). In older patients, both male and female, the therapist needs to be prepared to institute more of the environmental and milieu therapy and intervene with the purpose of offering a great deal of

---

N. Farberow and E. Shneidman, (1957) Suicide and Age. In E. Shneidman and N. Farberows, (eds.) *Clues to Suicide* (pp.41-49). New York: McGraw-Hill, Inc. (c) 1957 Reprinted by permission of McGraw Hill, Inc.

relief from physical pain and suffering. Sometimes it is necessary to provide analgesics and sedatives, and generally support is aimed at relieving feelings of discouragement, uselessness, and of possibly being a burden. This means the therapist may need to take a much more active part than generally when entering into the patient's environment in dealing with relatives and friends in helping to reestablish bonds of fading environment and lost feelings of usefulness and belonging. It seems this would be an appropriate approach in our present day treatment, perhaps with minor adjustments for the individual needs that are evident. In some cases, presently, it may mean establishing bonds with relatives and friends before considering reestablishing them, since some families have not had the opportunity to develop a bonded relationship because of the diverse lifestyle each member embraces. At any rate, there is a definite need for the person to have a feeling of belonging and to feel a sense of usefulness.

Assessing Suicide Potential

The importance of assessment and emergency evaluation for self-destructive potential was described by Litman and Farberow (1961). Mental health professionals are sometimes asked to make rapid assessments of an individual's self-destructive potential. Calls may come from the person him/herself or from a family member or friend. The role in answering such a request is threefold. First one needs to get the necessary information; then the professional person forms an evaluative judgment of the situation at hand, and finally that person makes a recommendation for appropriate action. Hospitalization is recommended in some cases for immediate attention; in other cases the suicidal communication is interpreted as a low lethality and the

---

R. Littman and N. Farberow. Emergency Evaluation of Self-Destructive Potentiality. In N. Farberow and E. Shneidman, eds. *The Cry for Help* pp. 48-77. New York: McGraw-Hill Book Co., (c) (1961). Reprinted by permission of McGraw-Hill, Inc.

recommendation for outpatient treatment may be the choice for intervention. In many cases it would be necessary to have additional interviews with a client with the aim of developing a more defined treatment plan. A systematic approach would include the most pertinent indicators of self destructive danger within a limited amount of time, in particular areas for data collection. The major areas for the short assessment for self-destructive potentiality included:

I.   Case history: factual

    A. Age and sex
    B. Onset of self-destructive behavior: chronic, repetitive pattern, or recent behavior change? Any prior suicide attempts or threats?
    C. Method of possible self-injury: availability, lethality?
    D. Recent loss of a loved person: death, separation, divorce?
    E. Medical symptoms: history of recent illness or surgery?
    F. Resources: available relatives or friends, financial status?

II.   Judgmental-evaluative

    A. Status of communication with patient
    B. Kinds of feeling expressed
    C. Reactions of referring person
    D. Personality status and diagnostic impression.

There is a continued need for increased adolescent study relating to their self-destructive behavior. Sadowski and Kelley (1993) noted limitations by definitions on their evaluation study to determine whether adolescent suicide attempters would have deficits in interpersonal problem-solving and the relation between social problem-solving, suicide intent and medical lethality. In comparison with psychiatric and normal controls, adolescents who attempted suicide exhibited poorer social problem-solving abilities, particularly in terms of problem orientation. The suicide attempters brought more maladaptive cognitive-emotional-behavioral response sets to problematic situations than did the psychiatric and normal controls. Social problem solving was not found to be correlated with suicide lethality or intent. The suicide attempters had poorer problem-orientation than distressed and nondistressed peers. The suicide attempter also reported a tendency to respond more emotionally in terms of positive and negative affect when they engaged in problem solving. They indicated they were more likely to adopt a stance of avoidance in response to problems, either putting off dealing with problems or looking for assistance from others. Behavior of avoidance, denial and dependency were evident.

In studying callers on two help lines in Los Angeles County over a two-week period, the sample was divided among adolescents, (ages 12-19 years), young adults (ages 20-26 years), and adults (ages 27 years and older). deAnda and Smith (1993) found that adults and young adults reported depression as their primary reason for contemplating suicide. The adolescents reported interpersonal problems for their reason. A small percentage fell into the high-risk categories with regard to the degree of planning suicide and the lethality of their chosen method.

Depressed individuals may be a greater risk for suicide if they live alone or do not have a stable relationship with a significant other. Males reported depression as the most frequent reason for contemplating suicide. Depression was second in frequency for females. Marital and love problems were first, along with combined relationships for females who considered suicide.

There were indications that the callers were white, female, and less than fully employed. Callers lacked a partner or spousal relationship or they were experiencing relationship problems. It would seem that the crisis line provides

---

D. deAnda and M.A. Smith. (1993) Differences Among Adolescent, Young Adult and Adult Callers of Suicide Help Lines, *Social Work, 38*, (4), 421-428. Reprinted by permission of the National Association of Social Workers, Inc.

and serves most frequently individuals troubled by ideation of suicide and infrequently the individuals at immediate risk for actually attempting suicide. Most positively, services from the help lines tip the caller's delicate cognitive and emotional balance toward selecting life and diffusing the crisis that might impel the individual into an extreme response. On the negative side, it appears that individuals who are at serious risk for suicide may not necessarily be attracted by the help line services. One characteristic of high-risk individuals is their resolve to commit suicide partially based on their belief that help is not possible in their particular situation. Perhaps educating the public regarding signs of risk for suicide and encouraging the use of help lines by individuals at risk and also the significant others would serve to help a larger portion of the population in need. For example, few male adolescents were found to use the help line. The adolescent girlfriends of males or sisters might consider seeking help from the help line in dealing with the at-risk male. It was noted from their findings there is a need to further explore within agencies the degree to which volunteers feel comfortable and competent to make referrals and feel committed to do so.

The importance of offering peer help line workers for troubled adolescents was demonstrated clearly by the study; adolescents had called the help line for teenagers. Because of the broad range of issues, it is suggested that "warm lines" that is help lines that focus on the adolescent's concern generally rather than primarily on suicide risk, might be more effective than hot lines.

PREVENTION - INTERVENTION

Some individuals attempt suicide and are considered as attention seekers rather than reaching out for help. It is reasonable and important to learn the motivation for any self-destructive act. When an adolescent is admitted to an institution for treatment it is critical that an assessment is made upon admission in order to take precautions, where necessary, to prevent the loss of life. The chance that intervention can occur is greater if the youth is in treatment, although intervention and treatment doesn't always prevent youths from committing suicide. (Lester, 1993).

Adolescents who made suicide attempts repeatedly were studied by Kolila and Lonnquist (1987), the study was completed in Helsinki, Finland. In comparing first time attempters with second time attempters (few multiples), repeaters were older than first-timers and normally no longer in school. Some of the more specific problems that were identified include: Underlying problems that were unsolved; Symptomatic failure in adaptation; Loneliness and being away from parents; Problems at home, at school and at work; Social isolation; Poor mental health; Girl and boyfriend problems; Unstable homes called chaotic; Separated parents and the threat of separation by some long before the occurrence of separation. The mean age of attempters was 17.6 (15-19 years of age) with females dominating the repeater group. Repeaters abused alcohol, medicine and illegal drugs more often than those who had not previously attempted. Repeaters committed crimes more often; their growth milieu was unsatisfactory, and repeaters seemed to suffer mainly from personality disorders.

The Borderline Personality Disorder

Factors that underlie the borderline personality disorder, whether constitutional predominantly or environmentally, primarily are of a nature as to render the suicide rate as high as that observed in the major psychoses. The

---

L. Kotila and J. Lonnquist. Adolescents who make suicide attempts repeatedly. *ACTA Psychiatr. Scand.*, 76: p. 386-393. By permission of the National Public Health Institute. Department of Mental Health, Helsinki. Finland (on behalf of Prof. Juoko Lonnquist).

individual is described as stormy, unstable, overanxious, anger-prone, impulsive, and destructive of self or others. Traits of the BPD include:

Impulsive: chaotic, fickle, desultory, flighty, inconstant, reckless, unpredictable;

Moody: mercurial, volatile;

Extreme: unreasonable, alternately adoring and contemptuous, childish, vehement, outrageous, unstable, creating "scenes";

Irritable: cranky, hostile, irascible;

Manipulative: demanding, importunate, possessive, seductive;

Dependent: clingy;

Lacking depth: without abiding interests, shallow; and

Vulnerable: fragile.

A decade ago, a number of family studies suggested that BPD was often associated with manic-depressive illness in the immediate family and could, in some instances, represent a dilute form of that condition. Others have noted the high incidence of depressive disorders in the close relatives of patients with other Axis II personality disorders, not just those with BPD. In some samples, a number of BPD patients have little in the way of environmental trauma but much in the way of bipolar/unipolar family members. Follow-up studies of borderline patients have been completed during the past five years.

There is a need for residential treatment in many fragile cases in order to provide care safely and effectively. It would seem that long-term residential care offers the most hope. In residential treatment, particularly among female BPD patients, the abuse factor, especially the incest factor, is important in

---

M. Stone (1990). Personal Reflections: Borderline Personality Disorder — Contemporary Issues in Nosology, Etiology, and Treatment. *Psychiatric Annals, 20*, (1), 8-10.

14

almost half of the cases. (Stone, 1990).

Black Youth Suicide

Suicide is a significant problem for black youths for more than one reason. It is a leading cause of mortality in this (15-24) age group, but also because it has a disproportionate impact on the black population. Their youthful population median age is 25.8 years, according to the U.S. Bureau of the Census, (1986).

Gibbs (1988) suggested there are too many blacks destroying themselves by suicide, homicide, or in fatal accidents, when they should be developing an identity, exploring career options, or beginning a family. Suicide is the third leading cause of death in black youths in the (15-24) age group, after homicides and accidents; and 47% of all black suicides occur in the (20-34) age group, according to the U.S. Bureau of the Census, 1986. The overall suicide rate of black youths (aged 15-24) has more than doubled in the past 25 years, with the males (20-24) accounting for most of that increase.

The three conceptual approaches used to explain suicide among black youths were: (1) the sociological approach; (2) the psychological approach, and (3) the ecological approach. Sociologically, the author applied Durkheim's (19th century French Sociologist), who proposed the three types of suicide, which related to lack of fit between the individual and society. As applied to this group, "anomic suicide" increases as the social integration individuals decreases, resulting in weaker social bonds and group norms; and society "fatalistic suicide" occurs when individuals cannot tolerate excessive social

---

J. Gibbs. (1988) Conceptual Methodological, and Sociocultural Issues in Black Youth Suicide: Implications for Assessment and Early Intervention. *Suicide and Life-Threatening Behavior, 18* (1), p. 73-89. Reprinted by permission of Guilford Press, New York, NY 10012.

restrictions and oppressive regulations. Concepts of "anomie," "social isolation," and "normlessness" may be applicable to all blacks who have been uprooted from the stable Southern rural area to mobile Northern urban or suburban society. They could predict higher suicide rates for older blacks, for those whom the impact of moving to a new environment is arguably even more traumatic than for younger people, but this is not the case. The sociological theories do not explain the differential suicide rates of black males and females, who we presume have similar environmental experiences in regards to changes and stressors, and yet they respond very differently. The psychological perspective can be traced from Freud's psychoanalytic concept that suicide represents anger resulting from the loss of a loved object, turned against the self (Freud, 1917/1925).

In many cases blacks lack networks of extended families, strong religious belief, alternative value systems, and alternative opportunity structures. Blacks migrated from the South in the 1930s and 1940s, leaving traditional communities. These institutions of family, church, community and extended kinship have been weakened significantly through urbanization, integration, massive social and economic change. Black youth and blacks generally were vulnerable to suicide.

Mobile black high school students are middle-class youths caught between parental pressures to achieve and peer pressure to conform to anti-intellectual norms. Black college students in integrated colleges have generally felt relegated to a very marginal role in social and extracurricular activities. More recently they have become targets of overt verbal and physical attacks at campuses as diverse as the University of Michigan. Deprivation also in the work world helps us to better understand why the middle-class and upper-middle class black youths appear to be committing suicide.

The Civil Rights Movement of the 1960s and 1970s raised their hopes and aspirations regarding opportunities. Expectations failed to materialize and they became frustrated, angry, and bitter. Some succumbed to depression and despair, followed by loss of confidence, and feelings of betrayal and anger at the system. According to Gibbs (1988) black males are more likely to be suspended from school; to be high school dropouts; to be arrested for delinquency; to become substance abusers; to become unemployed; and to be incarcerated more often than white males. The black males are also likely to die from homicide or accidents at a higher rate. Homicide and motor vehicle accidents are the leading causes of death for this group of the population.

Presuicidal behaviors of many black youths will initially be identified in school, in medical centers, by social welfare, and juvenile justice settings rather than in psychiatric settings. It is obviously imperative for professionals such as doctors, teachers, social workers, psychologists and psychiatrists to be aware of behavioral signs, physical symptoms, and life indicators, which are influenced heavily by the social and cultural context of young blacks' lives. It is evident there is a need for more empirical research to test some of the conflicting theories of black youth suicide.

Youthful Suicides

Beyond Jan-Tausch's initial study of 412 child and adolescent suicides, only six studies have attempted to delineate factors associated with self-inflicted death among younger persons in Western societies, (Jan-Tausch, 1964).

Hoberman (1988) reported the following methods of self-destruction in studying 656 youth suicides of children, adolescents and young adults. The younger group fell in ages (14-19 years); the older group encompassed (20-25 years) with male/female ratio (3:1).

Methods used:	Males	Females
Firearms	45%	17%
Hanging	16%	10%
Jumping	6%	12%
Ingestion	8%	31%
Carbon Monoxide	15%	11%
Suffocation	1%	1%
Other	8%	6%

Preciptants are listed in the upper limit of frequency to the lower limit, 15% to 2% - Arguments, Relation breakups, Problems with the Law, Disappointments, Work Problems, School Problems, Threats of Separation and Victims of Assault.

More recent suicides were more likely to be described as angry individuals. They were described as more likely to be in good health -- although a greater percent was described as having learning disabilities. White predominated; more suicides for young adults than adolescents; male, married, and separated appeared at greater risk for suicide; unemployed increased risk for recent suicides, and Native American males had a greater suicide percent than the white males.

Medical Legal Implications

The legal profession has rejected expert testimony of psychiatrists for decades. In the majority of federal and state courts, the prevailing opinion is that suicide is an intervening force which breaks chains of events from the time of the negligent act to the suicide subsequently. That was the favored viewpoint

---

H. Hoberman and B. Garfinkel (1988). Completed Suicide in Youth. *Canadian Journal of Psychiatry*, 33 (6), 494-502. Reprinted by Permission of *The Canadian Journal of Psychiatry*, (Ed. E. Kingstone, M.D.)

by the United States Supreme Court when it ruled that the proximate cause of a decedent's death was his suicide. It further ruled that the negligence of a defendant was too remote to justify recovery by the decedent's estate. Courts have chosen to rule as a matter of tort law, ignoring advances in psychiatry, ruling that suicide severs the chain of causation. English Rule requires that insanity result from injury itself or the shock that produced it, and not as an indirect cause resulting from brooding over the injury.

In recent workmen compensation cases and the trend that prevails in England there seems to be an inclination to accept the promise that psychiatry has not advanced to the point where it can reasonably determine etiology of the decedent's suicide. So, in this context suicide is viewed as a syndrome. It has a definite cause, consistent demographics, historical data that are specific, and clinical findings that are reproducible. With this information, a definite causality can be established and the outcome predicted with a high level of certainty. (Giannini, 1982).

As all other recognized illnesses, suicide has been shown to have both environmental and biological etiology. The sociological parameters of Durkheim (1897) are applicable, which could predict a suicide in a given individual under certain circumstances (Giannini, 1978). In the early twentieth century the study of new intrapsychic parameters enabled psychiatric physicians to draw a profile of an individual at high risk. This profile is the tool used routinely in hospital emergency rooms currently to assess a specific illness, including suicide (Giannini, 1983). With the above promises the medical approach to illness is constituted. Courts have accepted this approach in the form of other expert testimony. Therefore, it is maintained that it is inconsistent for the courts to reject this approach when applied to the syndrome of suicide (Giannini et al, 1989).

The biochemical study in regards to suicide is more exacting, more medical and more traditional than all other parameters. The identification of "'serotonin'" secreted by the brain can now be utilized as a biochemical marker identifying patients at suicidal risk (Giannini, 1989).

Co-Worker Intervention

Intervention is either a technique or a series of activities a therapeutic agent decides upon after thoughtful consideration of another human person and their affect, identification with the person and concern for the short-term and long-term goals, to help the person in need to attain a constructive outcome.

This interview by Mericle (1993) attempted to identify effect and reactions of a clinical nurse specialist whose colleague had committed suicide after their few months association in a psychiatric nursing experience.

The nurse interviewee reported having stages of feelings beginning with shock, anger, sadness and later guilt. She feared that she neglected being more helpful, since her co-worker did not appear depressed. Later she believed there was possibly depression present that she missed by treating her as a co-worker. There was a three-year period this psychiatric nurse used in detaching and working through the loss of her colleague. She began to work with the employee assistance program counselor, in how she could help staff. Therapists make the assumption too often that they must be strong and in control, rather than trying to find help for themselves to better accept and deal with loss -- especially loss by suicide. There needs to be a period of grieving when there is a loss (Merricle, 1993).

A. James Giannini, Matthew Giannini, and Andrew Slaby, (1989). The Medical Legal Implications. *The Psychiatric Forum*, p. 6-9. Reprinted by Permission of the Authors.

20

A Classroom Experience

The prevention program which bridges the field of practice with research knowledge was studied by (Ciffone, 1993). He maintained there are indications that their classroom program is effective, but does not claim this program is more effective than other programs. The program used an attitudinal survey for evaluation which has some limitation. One drawback is the implication that attitude and behavior are causally linked, which is not always true.

This educational program is in an Illinois high school which exposes all students as a required course in the sophomore health class to the topic of suicide. The teacher is assisted by a school social worker and they include a short video filmstrip depicting typical adolescents who are lonely and need to belong, which is a good basis for discussion and dialogue. Emphasis is on concern of the self-image, death as final, relationship between mental illness and suicide, and how to cope with loss-related stress. Listening skills are emphasized and attention is directed to school and community resources available to assist students in crisis. A positive self-esteem checklist is utilized which encourages the restoration of any feelings of positive self-esteem that may have been diminished by over-identification with the individual who attempted suicide in the video.

It was suggested that adolescents need to understand suicidal attempts and completions are probably symptoms of psychiatric illness which are treatable. It was apparent that a high proportion of adolescents had undesirable attitudes about suicide at the beginning of their program. The program appears to have caused a significant shift from undesirable to desirable attitudinal

J. Ciffone, (1993). Sucide Prevention: A Classroom Presentation to Adolescents. *Social Work*, v, 38 (2), 197-203. Reprinted by permission of The National Association of Social Workers, Inc.

responses in the majority of the targeted areas. Also the results seem to dispel a commonly held belief that associating mental illness with suicide will diminish self-disclosure.

Obviously, there is a need for further research and evaluation of programs to determine the measure of effectiveness in preventing suicide and other destructive behavior.

REFERENCES

Ciffone, J. (1993). Suicide Prevention: A Classroom Presentation to Adolescents. *Social Work* 38,(2), 197-203.

deAnda, D. and Smith, M.A. (1993). Differences among Adolescent, Young Adult, and Adult Callers of Suicide Help Lines. *Social Work*, 38, (4), 421-428.

Donne, J. (1982). *Biathanatos* (M. Rudick & M.P.Battin, trans.) New York: Garland. (Original work published 1644).

Durkheim, E. (1951). *Suicide A Study of Sociology* (J. Spaulding and G. Simpson, Trans.) New York: The Free Press. (Original work published 1897).

Farberow, N., and Shneidman, E. (1957). Suicide and Age. In Shneidman, E., and Farberow, N. (eds.), *Clues to Suicide*. (pp.41-49).

Freud, S. (1952). *Collected Papers* Vol.V. (edited by James Strachey) London: The Hogarth Press. (Original work published in 1917).

Giannini, A., Giannini, M., & Slaby, A. Suicide - The Medical Legal Implications (1989). *The Psychiatric Forum*, 6-9.

Gibbs, J. (1988). Conceptual Methodological, and Sociocultural Issues in Black Youth Suicide: Implications for Assessment and Early Intervention. *Suicide and Life-Threatening Behavior*, 18 (1), 73-89.

Haim, A. (1970). *Adolescent Suicide* (A.M. Smith, Trans.) New York: International Universities Press, Inc.

Henry, R., and Short, J., Jr. (1954). *Suicide and Homicide*. New York: The Free Press.

Hoberman, H., and Garfinkel, B. (1988). Completed Suicide in Youth. *Canadian Journal of Psychiatry*. 33, 494-502.

Jan-Tausch, J. (1964). *Suicide in Children 1960-1963).* Trenton New Jersey, N.J. Public Schools, Department of Education.

Kotila, L., and Lonnquist, J. (1987). Adolescents who make suicide attempts repeatedly. *Acta psychiatr. scand.* 76, 386-393.

Lester, D. (1993). *The Cruelest Death: The Enigma of Suicide.* Philadelphia: The Charles Press.

Litman, R., and Farberow, N. (1961). Emergency Evaluation of Self-Destructive Potentiality. In Farberow, N., and Shneidman, E. (eds.), *The Cry for Help* (pp.48-77). New York: McGraw Hill Book Company.

Mericle, B. (1993). When a Colleague Commits Suicide. *Journal of Psychosocial Nursing*, 31 (9), 11-13.

Sadowski, C., and Kelley, M. (1993). Social Problem Solving in Suicidal Adolescents. *Journal of Consulting and Clinical Psychology*, 61 (1), 121-127.

Stillion, J., McDowell, E., & May, J. (1989). *SUICIDE; Across The Life Span - PREMATURE EXITS.* New York: Hemisphere Publishing Corp.

Stone, M. (1990). Personal Reflections: Borderline Personality Disorder — Contemporary Issues in Nosology, Etiology, and Treatment. *Psychiatric Annals*, 20 (1), 8-10.

U.S. Bureau of the Census. (1986).

PART II

THE DEVELOPMENTAL AND LIFE PROCESSES

CHAPTER II

Theories of Normal Growth and Development

By
Carol Flaugher, M.S., RN.

The reader will become acquainted with the ramifications of psychosocial and cognitive development throughout the life span.

Development is often described as dynamic, meaning that it is ever changing. This ever-changing phenomenon leads to individual outcomes based on one's current developmental status and success with mastering the tasks of that particular level.

When one thinks of development, one often considers it as something happening only to children. However, development continues throughout the life span and its impact is felt by all individuals from infancy through old age.

Thus, we will examine this interactive process of psychosocial, cognitive and physical parameters as they affect an individual throughout the life span. The theories of Jean Piaget and Erik Erikson will provide the frame of reference for this examination.

Erikson's position reflects the belief that personality develops according to predetermined steps which are maturationally set. Kaplan (1988), in describing Erikson's premise, states that society is structured in such a way so as to invite and encourage the challenges that arise at particular times. Erikson (1968) refers to these challenges as developmental crises. He considers a healthy balance between two poles as a resolution to the crises at hand; although he feels that the outcome should tend toward the positive side.

Individuals striving for this healthy balance need to work through a variety of these developmental crises or tasks, in progression, to achieve a sense of comfort with themselves and their relationships with others. Erikson postulates that if an individual is not able to successfully master the crisis at hand, he will encounter remnants of its negative impact onward as he encounters further developmental tasks. An example of this would be reflected in the individual who has difficulty developing relationships with others because of his own difficulty with developing trust in others very early in his infancy.

The manner in which an individual perceives the world around him is largely influenced by his level of cognitive development. Children think differently than adolescents or adults because one's cognitive ability is dependent upon his level of development.

Piaget's theory proposes that cognitive development encompasses a series of stages, each of which requires some modification in the way individuals think. The ages at which the various stages are reached are normative, but may differ from person to person; the order of these stages is thought to be fixed.

Developmental changes described by both Erikson and Piaget are influenced by many biological, social, psychological, physical and cultural factors. Each culture has its own age norm that legislates behavior for specific age groups. This internalized sense of timing or SOCIAL CLOCK, guides individuals in terms of their progress with the social events in their lives. For instance, marriage at twelve or thirteen may be appropriate and expected in some cultures, whereas in others it may be frowned upon.

SOCIAL CLOCKS and age norms are affected by the historical period in which one lives. The experience of growing up in a particular time period exerts what is known as the COHORT EFFECT. Events that occur at one point in time, such as economic depressions, epidemics, and revolutions affect peoples' lives greatly. Thus, people in the same generation share common experiences. Children growing up during the depression arrive at adulthood with a different concept of finances than children growing up during times of affluence. When comparing people of different ages, the COHORT EFFECT must be taken into account.

Developmental implications are important to consider as one thinks about an individual at any point in time. How someone has responded to developmental tasks at hand will influence his current endeavors. As we consider the developmental theories of Erikson and Piaget, keep in mind the previously described elements of the SOCIAL CLOCK and the COHORT EFFECT.

Erikson's initial developmental crisis involves the development of TRUST. The infant who is reared in a positive, caring environment gradually comes to realize that there are those who consistently meet his needs. When this consistent pattern is perceived, the infant is said to have developed a sense of TRUST in himself and others. Inconsistency in caring patterns can lead the infant to feel MISTRUST which can impact on his ability to feel confident in his own worth and in his ability to relate to others as he grows through the life span. Thus, Erikson emphasizes that TRUST is the cornerstone of the child's attitude towards life.

During toddlerhood, the development of AUTONOMY is occurring as the child begins to utilize his newly acquired motor skills and basic language skills to learn about the world around him. At this time, caretakers are often faced with allowing the child freedom to explore while protecting him from his own lack of ability to maintain personal safety. A sense of self control without a loss of self esteem is the desired outcome of the developmental crisis facing this young child.

Erikson (1968) offers clarification of this stage as he states "the matter of mutual regulation between the adult and child now faces its most severe test. This time becomes decisive for the ratio between loving good will and hateful self insistence, between cooperation and willfulness and between self expression and compulsive self restraint. From an unavoidable sense of loss of self control and of parental over control comes a lasting propensity for DOUBT and SHAME."

Both parents and child are faced with issues of holding on and letting go. The parent must "hold on" or tend to the child for his own protection; but must "let go" to allow the child a chance to achieve autonomy. The child must "hold on" to what he wants to do in his attempt to assert autonomy; but must learn to "let go" of some of his will and submit to his parents without feeling a great deal of shame and doubt.

Being firmly convinced that he is a person on his own, the child of three or four years of age must now find out what kind of person he may become. Enhanced development of both language and locomotor skills allow the young preschooler the opportunity to explore his environment and to question those around him about all the curiosities in that environment. All this exploration and questioning leads to a sense of INITIATIVE as a basis for the child's sense of ambition and purpose.

Erikson (1968) calls GUILT the great governor of this INITIATIVE. He describes it as providing the necessary control on the child's literal intrusion into his environment. "With guilt", Erikson (1968) emphasizes, "a little is good for the sense of moderation it helps the child to achieve; too much is detrimental in that it can render the child totally inert." This new inner voice or conscience allows the child to begin to place limits on his own behavior rather than relying on the external sense of control which comes from his parents. As Erikson (1968) has described this newly developed conscience should exert only a moderate amount of GUILT. Being too critical of himself, the child can begin to experience nightmares and other negative feelings about himself.

School age children find it important to be productive. Their AUTONOMY has enhanced their sense of self; their INITIATIVE has encouraged them to relate positively to their environment. Now, as they move away from their family to the world of peers, teachers and other adult leaders, they have opportunities to begin projects and follow them through to completion, thus developing a sense of INDUSTRY or productivity. When unable to be productive, whether in a classroom assignment or any other activity, the schoolager develops a feeling of INFERIORITY or less capability than others. As with previous crises, the impact may continue to be felt into adolescence and adulthood.

Threats to the schoolager's self esteem continually pervade his mind. Jones (1985) presents the notion that in order to counterbalance this threat, children may develop behaviors which aid in the reduction of their anxiety and uphold a sense of self integrity. These anxiety-reducing behaviors are known as DEFENSE MECHANISMS. Many of them can persist into adulthood.

One of the more common DEFENSE MECHANISMS utilized by children is regression, retreating to an earlier form of behavior. Regression can be noted in the school age child who resumes thumbsucking or bed wetting at an anxiety-producing time; perhaps at the beginning of a new school year. The reader is encouraged to consult any number of psychology textbooks for further descriptions of the many existent defense mechanisms.

If a positive sense of INDUSTRY is achieved, the school age child will come away with a set of task identifications. Damon (1983) describes this as a set of beliefs in ones own ability to accomplish things and make things work. This is a direct precursor to the identity search of the adolescent because one's occupational choice is at the heart of one's personal identity.

The adolescent's rapidly developing physical being causes him to turn inward to take a look and begin to consider IDENTITY as a developmental issue. Cognitive developmental abilities now allow the adolescent to think about thinking. This leaves him open to a great deal of self examination and the possibility of a feeling of IDENTITY CONFUSION if he is not able to see who he really is.

Signs of a consolidated IDENTITY are an acceptance of oneself and one's actions, a feeling of comfort and appropriateness associated with one's self image and a general sense of psychosocial well being. The adolescent can satisfactorily say, "I am what I am."

Erikson states that the estrangement of this stage is IDENTITY CONFUSION. He sees this confusion of identity as the pervasive doubts that fall upon adolescents such as sexual insecurity, lack of autonomy and the inability to commit and give direction to their lives.

Erikson (1968) also writes that identity related psychopathology is one of the most common clinical disturbances in the first two decades of life. He adds that even much later in adulthood, many individuals experience conflicts that can be traced back to contradictions or insufficiencies in their identity resolutions.

In the process of identity formation, adolescents often look at themselves and imagine what others will think of them. However, a logical error occurs; they fail to differentiate between their own thoughts and the thoughts of others.

Being primarily concerned with themselves, adolescents believe everyone else is as obsessed with their behavior and appearance as they are. The inability to differentiate between what one is thinking and what others are thinking constitutes what David Elkind calls ADOLESCENT EGOCENTRISM. Elkind (1974) describes two interesting phenomena resulting from this ADOLESCENT EGOCENTRISM; IMAGINARY AUDIENCE AND PERSONAL FABLE. He recounts their peak at age thirteen and their ebb by age sixteen.

IMAGINARY AUDIENCE causes the adolescent to believe that everyone is looking at and evaluating him. People in the audience are real, but it is imaginary because most of the time the adolescent is not the focus of attention.

Elkind (1974) offers an explanation for this phenomenon, "Whenever the young adolescent is in public, he or she is - in his or her own mind - on stage playing before an interested critical audience."

According to Elkind (1974), the PERSONAL FABLE refers to two unique characteristics of adolescent thought: UNIQUENESS and INVINCIBILITY.

As the adolescent comes to reflect on his own thoughts, feelings and experiences, he begins to believe that what he is thinking and experiencing is absolutely unique and has never been experienced by another. Trusting in their own INVINCIBILITY, adolescents believe that they are immune from the laws of nature. A frequently held assumption is that it can't happen to me. Therefore one sees a great deal of risk taken during adolescence, without adequate thought to the reality of the situation.

For years many theorists considered adolescence to be the end of significant social, emotional and cognitive development. Erikson was one of the original theorists to recognize the significance of life span development and acknowledge its progression through older adulthood.

The young adult, usually one in his twenties or thirties is at a peak in relation to growth, strength and physical health. The focus of psychosocial development is now on INTIMACY. It is described as the ability to share emotional closeness with another. This may imply a marital relationship, but does include close friendship as well. The young adult who is not able to develop this emotional closeness is left with a feeling of ISOLATION, not relating at all to others or only being capable of superficial relationships. Some individuals may choose this isolation because it does not require the risk of being hurt in a relationship. Others are compelled to ISOLATION because of earlier difficulties with the development of trust.

Moving through adulthood one arrives at middle adulthood somewhere between the ages of forty and fifty. At this time the "decline" from the peaks of adulthood are beginning to be realized although they have been gradual, according to Berger (1988).

Erikson identifies the focus of development at this time to be on a sense of GENERATIVITY or productivity and a concern for the next generation. Those in middle adulthood now begin to sense their own mortality and want to leave their mark on society.

Being unable to be productive, for whatever reason, will leave the individual with a feeling of STAGNATION which then makes Erikson's final task of INTEGRITY extremely difficult to negotiate. The individual who is stagnated is described as literally stuck in his place in life with no motivation to move onward and no sense of being in the world.

Older individuals face their developmental crises and other life situations with less physical well being than others. The gradual decline of physical health and stamina may not even have been noticed as one aged through the twenties and into his fifties. Into one's sixties, Newman and Newman (1984) note that the individual is less resilient in the face of prolonged exertion. In addition, there is reduced speed in responding to stimuli, a slowing of motor response, reaction time, problem solving, memory and information processing.

Older adulthood is the time when the individual must develop a sense of EGO INTEGRITY or be left with a sense of DESPAIR. INTEGRITY is the positive outcome of the final stage of development. It is a sense of satisfaction with one's past and present life situation, giving the individual a sense of comfort in knowing that it was a good life, not to be changed or modified.

Not being able to feel this sense of INTEGRITY, the older adult is left with a feeling of DESPAIR or regret about his past and a continuing nagging desire to be able to do things differently. With despair, Newman and Newman (1984) state that one cannot resist speculating about how things might have been or about what actions might have been taken if only things had been different.

As presented at the beginning of this chapter, cognitive functioning is a vital parameter of one's development. It enhances or hinders the individual as he is attempting to master psychosocial developmental tasks across the life span.

Piaget described cognition as a process of adapting to the world around oneself. According to Piaget (1952), this ADAPTATION involves two processes: ASSIMILATION and ACCOMMODATION.

ASSIMILATION is the taking in process by which one incorporates new information into already existing patterns of behavior. Piaget refers to patterns of behavior as SCHEMA. For instance, the infant who has utilized sucking behavior to seek nourishment, will attempt to use the same behavior pattern or SCHEMA to take solid food from a spoon. When he finds that this behavior is not efficient he will accommodate or change his actions to fit the new situation. ACCOMMODATION thus is described as the process of shifting usual SCHEMA in order to encompass new information (Berger, 1988).

The SENSORIMOTOR PERIOD, Piaget's initial stage of cognitive development occurs from birth until about the age of two years of age. Changes during this time are dramatic in that the infant develops from functioning primarily on a reflex level to being capable of some goal directed behavior.

During this stage, the infant learns about his environment through the coordination of sensory input and motor activity. As Flavell (1985) states, "The infant exhibits a wholly practical, perceiving and doing, action bound kind of intellectual functioning: he does not exhibit the more contemplative, reflective, symbol manipulating kind we usually think of in connection with cognition."

The most important acquisition of this stage is the development of OBJECT PERMANENCE, the knowledge that an object has a permanent existence which is independent of one's perception of it. It's development proceeds slowly, but progressively, from a beginning awareness, around eight months of age, that objects might not disappear when they are out of sight to a full understanding of the concept at age two. Thus, the toddler who is expressing a need for AUTONOMY at this time can now move away from mother to explore his environment because he can carry a mental picture of his mother with him and know she exists outside of her immediate presence with him.

Language development enhances cognitive abilities from about the ages of two through seven. The child is now in Piaget's PREOPERATIONAL STAGE of development. He now begins to utilize language in place of the sensory and motor activities previously relied upon for ADAPTATION.

The reader is reminded that this age child is showing INITIATIVE in his psychosocial development as he begins an extensive use of his newly developed language skills to intrude upon his environment. Thinking of the three or four year old who continually asks "why", typifies this intrusion.

Despite his advances in cognitive abilities, the properitoneal child still experiences many obstacles or limitations to his thinking.

Piaget (1952) identified limitations that he felt impeded logical cognitive thinking in young children at this time. Some of the more critical limitations are EGOCENTRISM, CENTRATION and IRREVERSIBILITY.

EGOCENTRISM denotes the child's inability to consider another's point of view. Preoperational children think that everyone thinks the way they do and sees things they way they do. The typical four year old would see no need for further clarification when, from another room, he asks mother, "What is this?" He assumes she knows what he is talking about.

CENTRATION prohibits the child from considering the total essence of an object or a situation. Rather, he focuses only on one specific aspect which allows for many misinterpretations and illogical conclusions. Santa Claus can exist in the mind of the young child because of his only being able to focus on one aspect of the concept at a time.

The IRREVERSIBILITY of thought processes only permits the child to think in one direction. He cannot follow the line of reasoning back to its origin. Again, many misinterpretations and illogical conclusions can result. Kaplan (1988) presents a common example of this irreversible thinking. When a preschooler was asked whether he had a sister, he answered yes and gave her name. When asked whether his sister had a brother, he replied no.

As the child continues to grow and develop through the school age years, he now enters Piaget's Stage of CONCRETE OPERATIONS. During this time he develops the ability to apply logical thought to concrete problems. This school age child is no longer dominated by the previous limitations to his thinking as he moves into the world of peers and productive activity.

He now has the ability to assume another person's viewpoint. This serves to enhance his social interactions with peers. His thinking is no longer limited by CENTRATION and he can now consider the totality of an object or a situation. He is also able to reverse his thinking and be more aware of the sequencing of events.

In spite of all the gains, the schoolager's thinking is still limited to his own concrete experiences; he is not yet capable of dealing with abstractions. With the advent of the search for IDENTITY, the cognitive abilities of the adolescent reach their greatest level of development.

The adolescent is able to apply logic to all classes of problems. His thinking is characterized by the utilization of the scientific method, development of hypotheses and an advanced understanding of causation. He is also able to think about thinking as he moves from concrete thought to abstract conceptualization. Flavell (1985) clarifies adolescent cognition as he compares it to the school age child. He explains, "Before adolescence, the child has an earthbound, concrete, practical minded sort of problem solving approach and speculations about other possibilities occur only with difficulty and as a last resort. The adolescent and the adult by contrast, are more likely to approach problems quite the other way around with reality subordinated to possibility."

Egocentrism, however, reappears in adolescent thought. It is seen in the inability of the young adolescent to separate the real world from the idealistic. As previously discussed, this is evident in Elkind's descriptions of the IMAGINARY AUDIENCE and the PERSONAL FABLE.

Piaget did not believe that any further advances in cognitive development occurred beyond adolescence. However, he did admit that a person's life experiences and vocational endeavors are important factors in affecting the changes in cognitive functioning which can occur.

Over the past few decades, there has been an increasing interest in the cognitive functioning of adults. The impetus for this interest has come primarily from the increasing longevity of individuals.

Researchers are now looking at the impact of the aging process on cognitive thinking. Namely, those declining physical abilities previously described by New man and Newman. Theorists are not yet in agreement about the specific effects of these declines on cognitive abilities. Schale (1983) and Manton, Siegler and Woodbury (1986) however, indicate that declines in the cognitive functioning of older adults are related to change in their ability to process information rather than in their general knowledge capabilities.

In summary, it needs to be emphasized that an ages and stages approach to life span development does present a rather simplistic view. Seldom can an individual be so easily categorized. However, being aware of the general norms will allow one to know what to expect of individuals at various points in their life span.

REFERENCES

Berger, Kathleen (1988). *The developing person through the life span.* New York: Worth Publishers.

Damon, William (1983). *Social and personality development.* New York: W.W. Norton and Company.

Elkind, David (1974). *Children and adolescents: Interpretative essays on Jean Piaget.* New York: Oxford University Press.

Erikson, Eric (1968). *Identity: Youth and crisis.* New York: W.W. Norton and Company.

Flavell, John (1985). *Cognitive development.* Englewood Cliffs, New Jersey: Prentice-Hall.

Jones, Franklin, Garrison, Karl and Morgan, Raymond (1985). *The psychology of human development.* New York: Harper and Row Publishers.

Kaplan, Paul (1988). *The human odyssey: Life span development.* St. Paul: West Publishing Company.

Manton, Kenneth, Siegler, Ilene and Woodbury, Max (1986). Patterns of intellectual development in later life. *Journal of Gerontology*, 41, 486-499.

Newman, Barbara and Newman, Phillip (1984). *Development through life: A psychosocial approach.* Homewood, Illinois: The Dorsey Press.

Piaget, Jean (1952). *The origins of intelligence in children.* Margaret Cook (Trans.) New York: International University Press.

Schale, Warner (1983). *Longitudinal studies of adult psychological development.* New York: Guilford Press.

Schwartz, Steven and Johnson, James (1985). *Psychopathology of childhood: A clinical experimental approach.* New York: Pergamon Press.

CHAPTER III

The Wellness Concept

The Wellness Concept and Health

The Process

In discussing the status of one's health with someone you have not communicated with for a time, the description of your health may be stated as "good", or "I have been well", and "How are you?" This preface or introduction has been utilized almost like a ritualistic greeting by people for decades in our society.

Bruhn et al (1977) suggested that "good health" is not enough, because it may mean the absence of clinical signs of a disease only. Good health may imply a static or defensive position. Frequently it is seen as the consequence of little or no activity on the part of the individual in question and only results from avoiding illness-producing behaviors or circumstances. Actually good health is a continual process that hopefully will evolve into wellness.

Jourard (1974) stated man's view of his capacity to cope and survive, as well as grow, are critical factors in the development of life. Realizing one's own potential is of significance to one's health in continuing to change. Hence,

44

man is capable of experiencing more than good physical and mental health. Rather he can experience wellness and should actively seek to reexperience it throughout life.

Dunn (1959) explained that wellness is a process that continues in time, while good health is a state of being or stage along the health continuum. One can lose good health during illness, but maintain the potential for wellness always in some degree. Wellness is active rather than passive and it depends upon a person's initiative which requires the person's action, movement, development, decisions and value judgments. Good health on the other hand may exist without any effort on the part of the individual. Wellness, in this respect, is a response to one's potential for personal growth and it involves utilization of social, psychological, cultural, environmental, spiritual, and physiological resources which may well influence the potential of the individual.

Wellness is related to the processes of learning and development; tasks along the various points of development are cumulative and if factors that normally enhance wellness are absent or delayed, the potential for wellness is reduced.

Wellness and illness are at opposite ends of the health continuum, but are not mutually exclusive. For example, and individual may have an ache, pain, or a physical attack like appendicitis and yet experience wellness in the nonphysical aspects of life.

According to Ryan and Travis (1981) Wellness is a choice which is a decision you make to move toward optimal health; It is a way of life called lifestyle which you design to achieve your highest potential for well-being.

H.L. Dunn (1959). High-Level Wellness for Man and Society. *American Journal of Public Health* 49: 792-796. Copyright Holder: American Public Health Association. Reprinted by Permission of the American Public Health Association.

Wellness is a process, that is, a developing awareness that there is no end point, but that health and happiness are possible in each moment, here and now; It is an efficient channeling of energy received from the environment, transformed within you, and sent on to effect the world outside.

Wellness is the integration of body, mind and spirit -- the appreciation that everything you do, and think, and feel, and believe has an impact on your state of health; Wellness is the loving acceptance of yourself.

Thresholds of Wellness

Some individuals or families seem to pursue activities that promote wellness and avoid those that are believed to be illness-causing, and follow a lifestyle that encourages life enjoyment to its fullest. Other individuals or families may engage in behavior leading to good health only when symptoms of illness occur and later cease to continue this behavior once good health has been regained. The difference between circumstances in these two examples cited would seem to relate to their personal value systems and attitudes toward risk-taking learned in the developmental process. Developmental tasks are found in all cultures. Teaching and learning of these tasks implicitly or explicitly convey how individuals living in various cultures regard health, or the value they place on health. So, there are health-related tasks that are cross-cultural; and individuals have varying thresholds of wellness, and experience it in different ways. As a matter of fact, cultural patterns help in shaping uniqueness of the wellness process. Given their genetic inheritance and life circumstances, everyone has a different potential for wellness (Bruhn et al, 1977).

Individual Responsibility

One of the major aspects of holistic health from a personal perspective is self-responsibility in relation to health care. In earlier times most of the responsibility for health care and the process of attaining health was the physician's role and responsibility with a subordinate patient response in "doing what the doctor said".

Mattson (1982) stated that the principle of self-responsibility for health is one of the holistic health philosophy cornerstones, which places the control and accountability in the hands of the individual seeking care. Some high health-risk behaviors sited were smoking, overeating, and excessive use of alcohol. The person in question has responsibility to avoid these activities along with pursuing health promotion activities as exercise, relaxation, psychological awareness, proper nutrition, and spiritual questions. Most of the holistic techniques are considered both preventive and curative, along with a positive high energy well-being. The literature reflects the individual's potential for high-level wellness, radiant health, and self-fulfillment (Ardell, 1977; Shealy, 1977; Bloomfield, 1978; Travis, 1981). For some advocating the holistic health philosophy high-level wellness is the goal. When one gets sick, for example has a cold, the person needs to consider what was the predisposition or what led up to the illness, and what does the individual need to do to relieve the situation? Steps to correct the situation that helped to predispose the person to illness can be taken.

In case of a more serious illness there is a need to look into the psychological, spiritual, and possibly environmental origins. At the same time, the process may be essentially the same, with some thought as to unexpressed emotion which could be blocking energy flow, and causing the illness. Some believe the individual has responsibility for accidents, car trouble, personal misfortunes, and possibly genetic heritage.

Public health services have been directed to educate the public as to responsibility and preventive health practices by use of negative or fear conditioning, and usually have focused on a specific disease condition.

Mattson (1982) makes the distinction between holistic health and other "self-help" groups. Holistic health groups are usually not disease-oriented, but rather, growth-oriented.

The Illness/Wellness Continuum

Wellness is the right and privilege of everyone (Ryan and Travis 1981). There are degrees of wellness, as we know there are degrees of illness. People may lack physical symptoms, but they may be bored, depressed, tense, anxious or very unhappy with their lives. These emotional states may well set the stage for physical disease through the lowering of the body's resistance. They explainthat diseases and symptoms are not really the problem, but actually the body-mind's attempt to solve a problem   a message of the subconscious to the

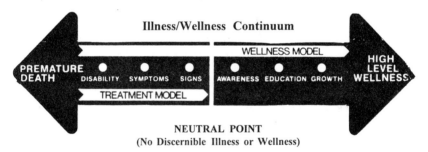

Illness/Wellness Continuum

NEUTRAL POINT
(No Discernible Illness or Wellness)

Moving from the center to the left shows a progressively worsening state of health. Moving to the right of center indicates increasing levels of health and well-being. The treatment model can bring you to the neutral point, where the symptoms of disease have been alleviated. The wellness model, which can be utilized at any point, directs you beyond neutral, and encourages you to move as far to the right as possible. If not meant to replace the treatment model on the left side of the continuum, but to work in harmony with it. If you are ill, then the treatment is important, but don't stop there.

R. Ryan and J. Travis (1981). *Wellness Workbook.* Berkeley, CA.: Ten Speed Press. Reprinted by Permission of Authors: 21489 ORR Springs Road, Ukiah, CA 95482.

48

conscious. Wellness extends the definition of health to encompass a process of awareness, education, and growth. Note in the illustration that The Illness/Wellness Continuum illustrates the relationship between the traditional medical model (or any other symptom-treatment system) and the wellness model, which is based on self-responsibility, as previously stated.

Ryan and Travis (1981) continued, wellness is like a bridge supported by two piers and each pier is crucial to the integrity of the bridge just as the two principles of self-responsibility and love are to the wellness process. The two create the pathway between the two distant (or contrasting) points, allowing for movement back and forth. It is the balanced flow between contrasting positions, attitudes or emotions, rather than attachment to any particular one, which defines maintaining balance and integrity. If either principle is weakened, the crossing may get scary; when both self responsibility and love are strong, energy flows freely.

Wellness for the Elderly

There have been so many progressive changes in the last century with new knowledge regarding sanitation and public health, and the progress of diagnostic medicine, antibiotic therapy, and immunization, that suffering and premature death have been eliminated to a large degree. Throughout history major illness and death resulted from natural disasters, infant mortality, and many infectious diseases like, pneumonia, influenza, diphtheria, tuberculosis,

---

K. Dychtwald (1986). *Wellness and Health Promotion for the Elderly.* (ed.) Ken Dychtwald of Dychtwald and Associates, Berkeley, CA. Rockville, MD: An Aspen Publication. (Out of Print) Reprinted by Permission of Aspen Publishers, Inc.

S.N. Walker (1992), Wellness for Elders. *Holistic Nursing Practice*, 7 (1). 38-45. Reprinted by Permission of Aspen Publishers, Inc.

cholera, and smallpox. The average life expectancy has been increased to correspond to these advances. To offset the infectious illnesses in the twentieth century, society has experienced a dramatic rise in the incidence of stress and life-style-related chronic degenerative diseases. Primary killers include, heart disease, cancer, strokes, accidents, cirrhosis of the liver, and diabetes. The high incidence of these noninfectious diseases are more reflective of unhealthy lifestyles than other factors, and they have become primary obstacles to high levels of health and long life among many of the older population.

The breakthroughs in genetic engineering, biopharmacology, organ transplantation, and reconstructive surgery, we can see the time when much of the age-related physical degeneration and illness will be a thing of the past.

As life expectancy continues to increase, the number and percentage of older Americans will continue to grow, particularly in the upper age categories. Increasing numbers of Americans will expect and plan to live a long healthy life span of nine, ten, or more decades (Dychtwald, 1986).

Promotion of Wellness

The growing awareness of the importance of health promotion with older adults was evident in the U.S. Surgeon General's 1988 Workshop on Health Promotion and Aging.

Gerontological nursing has always been concerned and defined by a focus on promoting health and function with older adults.

Interpersonal Support

Walker (1992) described healthy interactions with others as a component of a wellness lifestyle. It is important to maintain relationship involving a sense of warmth, intimacy, and closeness. People have a need to have someone with whom they can confide and to share joys as well as concerns. They need the experience of connectedness associated with touching and being touched. The older people lose family and close friends and experience geographic distancing of their children. It may well be necessary to develop new sources of support as familiar ones are lost. The senior centers, church groups, community volunteer opportunities, and educational programs for older adults or for any age may be helpful for many. Health, personal care, and social services available from agencies of the aging network to community-living elders are vital to the enhancement of wellness by increasing options for personal lifestyle choices.

Self-actualization

Self-actualization or spiritual growth may be most central to wellness (Walker, 1992). It involves experiencing awareness of and satisfaction with self, having a sense of purpose in life, and continuing to grow and develop as a person. This is a time in later years to look back and establish new goals for the remainder of life. Some earlier unfulfilled dreams may be realized through unique personal means. Nurses provide role models for a wellness lifestyle by teaching people about options. Nurses do this through their manner of caring, through empathy, and love.

Symptom assessment and intervention - a holistic approach

Vessey and Richardson (1993) identified factors in making holistic assessments of clients. In addition to culture, gender, personality, health beliefs, and socioeconomic status, they elaborated on the incorporation of the client's developmental stage as part of the assessment. If the care provider categorizes the young mother client as an adolescent who cannot cope with tasks of mothering, she/he may misdiagnose the complaint of the infant. The young mother described the child as feeding poorly and the child cried "too much and too shrilly". The nurse provider asked for clarification and details of the infant's cry, eating and sleeping patterns, temperature level, and other subtle changes which led to diagnosing a condition using the developmental level of both the mother and the child. The infant's diagnosis of meningitis was a life-saving intervention.

Environmental factors explored noted reductionism in the infrastructure of the present health care system contributing to problems dealing with client's symptomatology. Clients do not always have a long-term contact with the provider because of lack of insurance, poor access to care, personal health beliefs, and fragmentation of the health care system.

Clients have difficulty finding anyone who can or will examine their symptoms from a holistic perspective mostly due to increased specialization. Nurses are in an ideal position to view clients holistically and to coordinate their care, but they are also becoming more specialized as the health care system defines their practice. Appointments in health care facilities are fixed at short intervals well in advance of the appointment date. Also, reimbursement from third party insurers requires a diagnosis, where clients often present vague signs and symptoms, making an immediate diagnosis difficult.

The partial solution for a holistic care approach involves a multidisciplinary case conference or symptom management teams to ensure communication, care, and creativity in symptom management. Early referral to appropriate providers as the clinical nurse specialist or interdisciplinary teams would be beneficial. They recommend that through communication, caring, and

J.A. Vessey and B.L. Richardson (1993). *A Holistic Approach to Symptom Assessment and Intervention*. Holistic Nursing Practice, 7 (2) 13-21. With permission of Aspen Publishers, Inc.

creativity providers can interpret symptomatology as a congruent whole. Only then can providers create solutions for effective management of clients' symptoms.

REFERENCES

American Nurses' Association. (1987). *Standards and Scope of Gerontological Practice*. Kansas City, MO: ANA.

Bruhn, J., Cordova, F., Williams, Fuentes, R.,Jr. (1977). The Wellness Process. *Journal of Community Health*, 2 (3), 209-221.

Dychtwald, K. (1986). *Wellness and Health Promotion for the Elderly*. (Ed. Ken Dychtwald of Dychtwald & Associates,   Berkeley, CA.) Rockville, MD: An Aspen Publication.

Jourard, SM (1974). *Personality: An Approach from the Viewpoint of Humanistic Psychology*. New York: MacMillan.

Mattson, P. (1982). *Holistic Health in Perspective*. Palo Alto, CA: Mayfield Publishing Company.

Ryan, R., and Travis, J. (1981). *Wellness Workbook*. Berkeley,   CA: Ten Speed Press.

U.S. Dept of Health and Human Services, Public Health Service. *Proceedings of the Surgeon General's Workshop, Health Promotion and Aging*, Washington, D.C.: U.S. Government Printing Office.

Vessey, J., and Richardson, B. (1993). A holistic approach to symptom assessment and intervention. *Holistic Nurse Practice*, 7, (2) 13-21.

Walker, S. (1992). Wellness for Elders. *Holistic Nursing Practice*, 7 (1), 38-45.

CHAPTER IV

LIFESTYLES
Effects on the Family and Society

Basic Experiences

The pattern of living one's life generally begins in the family, and the maturation of a child in the family depends to some degree on the mother and her development as a woman. The senses seem to take in what feels good in the environment or social surround. Physical behavior progresses as the identification process takes place, followed by assimilation or introjection into what finally becomes a person who feels respect for role models, has an awareness and a sense of discipline -- a dimension of authority figures. The sensitivity of the organism to stimuli and re-enforcement from parents, siblings and others moves on toward developing and embracing the lifestyle he/she will eventually accept. That pattern may remain static for some time, but will change when a purposeful need is realized to create an alteration in the pattern.

Family Influence

The family has the first opportunity to make an impact on the psychosocial growth and development of a person, but with the changing family work patterns that have evolved particularly for women, the Day Care personnel and other children are creating additional effects on the individual child.

For many reasons, including one-parent families, the mother works outside the home on a regular basis. She may be the only source of financial support for her child and for herself which necessitates a changed pattern for the pre-school child. It may be viewed as a more stressful experience than with a two-parent home, but the future will provide information that could prove a positive influence on the child. This may lessen the era of dependency somewhat and it may strengthen the independency of the individual at an earlier stage of development.

Role of American Women

The increased labor force of wives is often viewed as a major sign of the changing role of some; some of the pattern change has to do with the role conflict as well as financial need. Wifehood and motherhood are not necessarily viewed as the woman's only career or occupational choice, hence, the expanding boundaries beyond the home. The working wife is currently recognized as a legitimate client population and is lost in the label of "'deviant'".

The home and job pose some conflicting demands and expectations which require some adaptation for all involved. One position holds that work buffers wives from the stresses of life, and that position is becoming quite popular. At the same time, there is some relinquishing of the mothering role as the children become more self-sufficient and some leave home. Old ways are frowned on as new political and social ideology emerge. Housewives were sometimes considered victims of the traditional ideology. Attacks on housework and on housewives may continue and even elevate the status of employed wives, but they do so at the expense of some who may prefer the traditional way of life

(Iglehart, 1980).

B. Bullough (1973) described women as never holding a position of equality with men, nor have they been viewed in that position by themselves or their menfolks.   Physical strength was a significant variable in the early development of our society, which helped to establish the subordinate position of women.   The nature of the reproductive processes and responsibilities in caring for the offspring kept women at a disadvantage in the work world, which carries higher status in most societies.   Once the discriminatory pattern of males as superior and girls as inferior was setup, it was carried forward by the socialization process.   Part of the belief that there were psychological and intellectual differences between men and women, led to females not having the right to pursue higher education, or be involved in the political arena.

Today, it is obvious that women are moving forward more intently in educational endeavors and definitely they are involved in politics.   Currently, women are beginning to be permitted to serve actively in combat in some divisions of the armed forces.   These freedoms are obvious in many parts of the world.

Infancy and Adaptation

Adaptive techniques must be acquired by the infant, handed down by society's culture as a supplement to the child's inborn endowment.   These techniques in a workable pattern must not be left to chance.   The child has a

---

A. Iglehart (1980). Wives, Work, and Social Change: What about the Housewives? *Social Service Review* by The University of Chicago. (September 1980). Reprinted by Permission of The University of Chicago Press.

B. Bullough (1973). *The Subordinate Sex* In Vern L. Bullough (Ed.). (Chicago: University of Illinois Press. pp. 335-338. Reprinted by permission of author.

58

prolonged need for nurturant care. With innate potentialities, it is necessary to structure, direct, and delimit activities in order for the individual to later become capable and adaptable to society as an integrated person. This person will then at a later stage transmit ways to the following generations.

The family forms a shelter for its members within a society and protects children from other members of society, mediating between the child's biological needs and societal directives. The family institution seems to be the most powerful and most effective arrangement, where conscious design and unceasing love are ruling (Lidz, 1968).

School and Task identification

At school age, (Erikson, 1968) described task identification. At the completion of the expansive imagination period or school age, the child is ready to learn more quickly and has a sense of sharing obligation, discipline and performance. The child is also eager to make things together with others, to share in constructing and planning. Children soon attach themselves to teachers, to parents, and to other children. They watch and imitate people representing occupations which they can grasp, for example, firemen, policemen or others. The child gains knowledge related to basic skills of simple technologies, which help prepare him/her to handle utensils, tools and even weapons as used by big people. The child enters the technology of the tribe gradually but directly. More literate people with more specialized careers, must prepare the child by

---

E. Erikson (1968). *Identity Youth and Crisis*. New York: W.W. Norton & Company, Inc. Reprinted by Permission of W.W. Norton and Company.E. Erikson (1968). *Identity Youth and Crisis*. New York: W.W. Norton & Company, Inc. Reprinted by Permission of W.W. Norton and Company.

Theodore Lidz (1968). *THE PERSON - His Development Throughout the Life Cycle*. New York: Basic Books, Inc., (c) (1968, 1972, 1982). Reprinted by Permission of Basic Books, A Division of Harper Collins Publishers, Inc.

teaching things which make them literate. Then the child is exposed to and given the widest possible basic education for the greatest number of possible careers (Lidz, 1968).

Children become dissatisfied and disgruntled without a sense of being able to make things well and even perfectly, referred to as sense of industry (Erikson, 1968). Although there has been a time provision as diversion in play or make-belief of games, without productive experiences, the best-entertained child soon acts exploited. It is as if one is psychologically a rudimentary parent already and one who must begin to be something of a worker and potential provider before becoming a biological parent. The advancing child quietly "'sublimates'" during the latency period before puberty and begins to apply concrete pursuits and approval goals -- the drives which have caused dreams and play. The person develops perseverance and adjusts the self to the inorganic laws of the tool world.

Teachers

It is important that teachers are wisely chosen for their abilities and for their caring for children.

Erikson (1968) suggested that good teachers who feel trusted and respected by the community know how to alternate play and work; games and study appropriately. They also know how to recognize special talents and provide encouragement for the gifted. Good parents feel a need to encourage their children to trust their teachers who can be trusted. The development and maintenance of a positive identification with those who know things and know how to do things is important for children. The knowledgeable teacher knows how to encourage the learner without creating identity confusion. The key, apparently, is stimulating the self-fulfillment in the child, which surpasses the fixation at the "good little worker" or "good little helper" stage.

Early Adolescent Females

An important preface to lifestyle has to do with how relationships form and develop among adolescents. It has already been suggested that much behavior is affected by traditional patterns and re-enforced by role models for an extended period of an individual's life. The identification process motivated by professional role models is common past the adolescent stage of development. In the American society love seems to be an emotion that is important which is defined and frequently redefined with additional life experiences.

Simon, Eder, and Evans (1992) relate that little attention has been directed toward learning how adolescent females acquire basic cultural knowledge about romantic love or norms to guide romantic feelings. This research examined underlying romantic love among early adolescent females. It is apparent from previous research that romance and male-female relationships are especially important to white adolescent girls. The interest that girls have of being attractive and popular replace their earlier concerns with academic and athletic achievement.

Feeling Norms Underlying Romantic Love in Adolescent Female Peer Culture were identified as following:

1. *Romantic relationships should be important, but not everything   in life.*
2. *One should have romantic feelings only for someone of the opposite sex.*
3. *One should not have romantic feelings for a boy who is already attached.*

R. Simon, D. Eder, and C. Evans (1992). The Development of Feeling Norms Underlying Romantic Love among Adolescent Females. *Social Psychology Quarterly*, 55 (1), 29-46. Reprinted by Permission of The American Sociological Association and the Authors.

4. *One should have romantic feelings for only one boy at a time.*

5. *One should always be in love.*

Data were collected as part of an ethnographic study of adolescent socialization and peer interaction in a middle school. The selected school was located in a medium-sized western community, enrolling sixth-, seventh-, and eighth- grade students from a range of socioeconomic backgrounds. Youths were from upper-middle class and lower working-class families. Most of the students were white, with a small number of black youths enrolled. Each grade had approximately 250 students enrolled.

Peer interaction and relationship data were collected over a three-year period and involved a variety of methods, including participant observation, audio and audiovisual recording and group interviews of some depth. By the seventh and eighth grades, norms concerning the relative importance of romantic relationships as well as the appropriate object of romantic feelings had emerged in these groups considered friends.

It was found in this study that adolescent girls used a variety of communication strategies to communicate normative information and to reenforce emotion norms to friends. They learned from each other about feeling and expression through light and playful language activities along with serious and confrontive modes of discourse. A more common strategy was use of humor, like by joking and teasing remarks, group members could point out to their friends norm violations in a non-threatening manner. Girls often used gossip and confrontations to clarify and reenforce feeling norms. It was noted that some group members revealed resistance and defied the group's feeling and expressing norms.

Romance is highly salient since having a boyfriend enhances girls' popularity with peers, particularly if it is important for their self-image.

62

Two norms that emerged were, concerning relative importance of romantic relationships and importance of being in love continually. Perhaps after romantic relationships become tied less closely to the peer group status, females feel they want to continue with a romantic relationship with a male, to validate their attractiveness and worth to self and others. The question posed outside the study focus of peers, asked to what extent do children acquire normative information about romantic feelings from members of an immediate family and cousins? It is suggested that girls may also acquire cultural knowledge about love through romantic films, novels, and television.

This study did not focus on the socialization of males. The different approach to romantic socialization of adolescent males may well differ, while it is also possible that they, too, utilize some of the same discourse strategies as used by females (Simon et al, 1992).

Life Experiences and Their Influence

Life and development of the human person does not occur in a vacuum. Through the life experiences of school at all levels, relationships with family members and family friends, and eventually associates in the work place, all have a potential effect on the lifestyle of another. What actually happens, an individual is exposed to habits and habit patterns of others on a continuing basis.

Burnham (1993) describes the history of American bad habits, in which he includes, cigarettes, whiskey, and wild, wild women, summed up and entitled:

J.C. Burnham (1993). *BAD HABITS*. New York: New York University Press. Reprinted with Permission of New York University, Ohio State University Alumni Association, Inc., and the Author.

BAD HABITS.

In exploring influences of vices on American society throughout history, the researcher anticipated finding out why many "good" people engage in activities including themselves that many consider "bad". In reality, the researcher found a coalition of economic and social interests in which the single-minded quest for profit allied with values of the Victorian saloon underworld and bohemian rebelliousness. The combination, he believes, radically inverted common American standards of personal conduct.

Drinking, smoking, sexual behavior, taking drugs, gambling, and swearing are labelled vices and yet they have been traditionally considered attractive, recreational, and gratifying activities. The bad habits possessed and still possess a fundamental attribute: they have ritualistic aspects. Users of tobacco have from the beginning tended to consume it in a repetitive way over and over. The bad habits from the nineteenth century on, were ritual transgressions subject to moral judgment.

In the twentieth century, indulging in minor vices produced intense social effects that endowed them with another kind of cultural significance, that may be more serious than originally anticipated.

Smoking is different from drinking, but the two are frequently associated and both have continued into the twentieth century. Smoking even before the nineteenth century had become the stigma of a "'bad habit'", offensive as a health hazard, manners, and thrift. It also took on a gender connotation, in that men smoked and chewed. Through advertising in the twentieth century the industry and users were pulled to support and contribute to the other bad habits, and cultural changes helped them prosper.

When World War II came, social pressure to smoke was overwhelming. Cigarettes were given out free with rations for soldiers and tobacco farmers were exempted from the draft because they were "'essential'" workers. After Rosie the Riveter appeared with a cigarette in her hand or between her lips, pressure was on for women to smoke. By the end of WWII, the percentage of American women who smoked doubled.

An Inversion of Values

American values turned upside down in the twentieth century (Burnham, 1993). Although there is some indication of change and transformation in the early 1920's, but more recently witnesses believe the real change occurred after midcentury.

In regards to marriage and parenthood there was some change around 1979. Today marriage and parenthood are rarely viewed as necessary, and those people who do not choose these roles are no longer considered socially deviant. Moral righteousness went out of style. A 'no restraint' standard came into vogue, particularly relating to bad habits.

Sexual Misbehavior

Americans from colonial days to the late twentieth century believed that sexual activity outside of conventional monogamous marriage constituted misbehavior on some level at least. Even the glamour of gambling would have been diminished without its association with prostitution and other sexual activity in places like the Las Vegas casinos. From the late 1979 on, pornography outlets offered dirty books and movies, and frequently prostitution, drug dealing, gambling, and other criminal activities. It has been noted by the researcher and author that these supermarkets of vice which were organized around a symbol of sexual misbehavior, even accepted major credit cards... Eventually the mass media found it profitable to exploit ideas about misbehaving sexually that moved American attitudes and standards toward a model which originated in small-time pornography and prostitution . . .

Drinking

The business of alcoholic-beverages, before and after Prohibition, influenced the ways in which Americans used their leisure time and socialized with each other. Supporters of drinking painted an unfavorable picture of prohibition laws. In the era of mass media, advocates moved into advertising. After 1933, alcoholic-beverage vendors and allies emphasized lifestyle advertising and implied other problems connected with drink were difficulties of the individual and was not a social problem.

Swearing

This was different from the other vices, and the use of offensive language involved no overt behavior outside verbal communication. By the 1920's and 1930's, a powerful group had been added to those Americans who favored swearing and they were the journalists, and later, media people of other varieties under the banners of fighting censorship, which they generalized from politics to all areas of life. In 1939, some journalists praised moviegoers on their sophistication when a character used "'damn'" as in the movie, ' Gone With the Wind'. All in all, continued agitation led many Americans to view increasing latitude of expression as real progress. By the late 1930's, journalists portrayed formal opponents of swearing as only quaint eccentrics.

Gambling

Wagering is known in most human cultures, but gambling in America has been considered a bad habit. Similar to drug taking, gambling undermined the work ethic and embodied danger of addiction. Crime stories through the years, nineteenth century particularly, emphasized loss of money wagering made those people subject to a temptation to steal. Over generations, Americans continued to connect betting with bad character. Most Americans of the late twentieth century have been unaware that minor vices have continued to have social, and historical significant effect on our society.

In reviewing these so-called bad habits described by Burnham (1993) it is as if a few individuals follow personal inclinations to meet their basic wishes with little or no concern as to how their behavior might affect others in society. These behaviors become more and more attractive to more individuals who want to respond to their basic wants rather than needs. So, after a time, these habits once believed to be vices, that were unacceptable by the vast majority of people, begin to be tolerated and almost considered acceptable behavior by many in that same society (Burnham, 1993).

We could possibly anticipate that, in the absence of self discipline with few identified restraints or external discipline from family and community, our present affluent society might well ignore its talents and future capabilities for constructive behaviors, and live a more hedonistic lifestyle.

REFERENCES

Chapter IV

Bullough, B. (1973). *The Subordinate Sex* In Vern L. Bullough (Ed) (Chicago: University of Illinois Press), 335-338.

Burnham, J. (1993). *BAD HABITS.* New York: New York University Press.

Erikson, E. (1968). *Identity Youth and Crisis.* New York: W.W. Norton & Company, Inc.

Iglehart, A. (1980). Wives, Work, and Social Change: What about the Housewives?" *Social Service Review* by The University of Chicago.

Lidz, T. (1968). *THE PERSON - His Development throughout the Life Cycle.* New York: Basic Books, Inc

Simon, R., Eder, D., and Evans, C. (1992). The Development of Feeling Norms Underlying Romantic Love among Adolescent Females. *Social Psychology Quarterly*, 55 (1), 29-46.

CHAPTER V

How to Develop a Healthy Self Concept

Development of a Healthy Self-Concept

How you feel about yourself is very important!

Feelings and attitudes about the self have a definite relationship as to your choice of a career, and once the choice is made, how you maintain a positive self-esteem with your choice through life experiences.

The psyche is not stationary but rather it is dynamically moving with day-to-day activities and encounters. The positive evaluations of life experiences need to be emphasized and the life stressors need to be de-emphasized and put in perspective. It is the belief of some theorists that the self-concept continues to develop over a lifetime.

Definition of Terms

Self-Concept refers to the collection of personal attributes by which an individual describes or characterizes the self, (or gives a description of self)

Theodore Lidz (1968). *The PERSON: His Development Throughout the Life Cycle.* New York: Basic Books, Inc., Publishers. (c) (1968, 1972, 1983). Reprinted by Permission of Basic Books, Division of Harper Collins Publishers.

(Beane et al,1980).

Self-Esteem refers to the relative value one attaches to the self-concept descriptors. It is the judgment of the value worth of self, realizing that self-esteem judgments are made on the basis of those values which the person holds. (Beane et al, 1980).

It will not be necessary to redefine growth and development as a specific theory related to one's self-concept development but rather to identify ways of determining the change of self-concept and maintenance of a healthy self-esteem from more than one theoretical framework.

According to Lidz (1968) the family has more responsibility for the child's development than enculturation. In order for the infant to become an integrated and a reasonably independent adult, he/she needs to be nurtured and enculturated, but the integration as a person must be directed by the family in which he/she is reared. As a small group, each member is affected by reactions and counteractions of the other members, and there is a need for them to find reciprocal interrelating roles to avoid distortion of personalities. At times the group requires a certain degree of precedence over wishes and possibly needs of individual members. For the child, the family serves as the primary social group upon which all subsequent group and interpersonal relationships are founded.

Nurturance is more than meeting the child's needs but it involves the emotional needs for love, affection, and a sense of security; it also includes providing opportunity for the individual to utilize new capacities as maturation takes place. The parents must know and feel when there is need for altering their ways of relating to the child with changing needs.

The quality and nature of parental nurturance will profoundly influence emotional development, i.e., vulnerability to frustration, the aggression, anxiety, hopelessness, anger, and helplessness experienced under various conditions. This re-enforces what Erikson described as development of basic trust for others and in himself. It influences a sense of autonomy while clarifying boundaries established between the child and parents. This nurturance contributes to the child's self-esteem as a member of his/her own sex. It further lays the foundations for trust in the reliability of collaboration and value of verbal communication as a way of problem solving.

It is very important for the parents to form a working coalition to establish the individual family position and responsibility to maintain stability and a feeling of well-being in the child. A coalition helps the parents to deal more effectively with the individual child as rivalries and jealousies evolve normally. Directives from both parents are internalized and each child identifies to a greater or lesser degree with each parent. When parents are reconcilable in dealing with the child there is less chance for conflicts in motivations, directives, and standards necessary to achieve an integrated personality (Lidz, 1968).

There is some agreement among theorists that "family" is at the heart of the concept of self development. This topic is particularly relevant in our current times, nearing the end of the twentieth century, when families in our Western world are frequently struggling with effects of separations of spouses and divorce that very often become permanent separations.

Turner and Helms (1979) described the child's self-concept development consisting in part of evaluation of the degree to which personal attributes compare with those the culture conceives as "good" or "acceptable," like warmth, honesty, intelligence, physical attractiveness, wealth, power, and a

---

J. Turner and D. Helms (1979). *Life Span Development*, Orlando, FL.: Holt, Rinehart and Winston, Inc., pp. 157-158. Reprinted by Permission of Holt, Rinehart and Winston, Inc.

capacity for enjoying life. Social experiences will determine to what degree children feel they possess these "good" attributes. Power and/or strength, for example, may be best determined by defeating a rival, resisting pressure, or dominating others. Children are prone to perceive themselves positively or negatively on the basis of their identification with various models. Identification is distinguished from imitation in that it is a motivational disposition rather than an instrumental response. Identification is maintained without obvious extrinsic or situational rewards, and the individual's similarity to the models persists during absence of the models.

Sarbin (1954) defines *self* as those ideas the individual has of himself which he has learned in relationship with others, and *role* as organized actions of a person coordinated with a given position or status. Self and role interact since the self strives for consistency and selects those roles compatible with the self-concept, and those role experiences, in turn, either do or do not reinforce the concept of the self. When the self-concept and the role are incompatible, conflict arises. The self-concept is not only, in part, a product of social roles, but also seems to be a major determinant of occupational role-taking, that is, of occupational choice. People tend to view a vocation as favorable or unfavorable for them because their ideas of that occupation either do or do not fit into their concept of themselves. Sarbin, (1954).

According to Sullivan, "The self may be said to be made up of reflected appraisals. If these were chiefly derogatory . . . then the self dynamism will itself be chiefly derogatory . . . it will entertain disparaging and hostile appraisals of itself" . . . "the self tends very strongly to maintain the direction

---

T. Sarbin (1954). *Handbook of Social Psychology.* (Eds.) G. Lindzey and E. Aronson. Cambridge, MA: Addison-Wesley Publishing Co. Reprinted by Permission of McGraw-Hill, Inc., New York, N.Y.

and characteristics given it in childhood" (Sullivan, 1947).

Ego psychologists, following a concept introduced by Erikson, considered young adulthood an important period for stabilizing the ego-identity. Work of the ego in the young adult is to create balance between the id impulses of early childhood and the powerful superego from parental values, and to blend the self-conceptions of others into a sense of identity. "A critical factor in establishing a sense of self or identify, and perhaps one of the most difficult tasks of young adulthood, involves the emancipation from family controls and detachment from parents or parental representatives" (Meyer, 1973).

Lyell (1973) suggested that the "sense of identity is disturbed at adolescence because the 'what he does' is not culturally valued". Elders are indifferent to what he thinks and does; he is rarely approached for his approval or acceptance, tolerated or ignored or taken seriously only by his peers -- all because the activities of adolescents are not culturally valued. Mostly the adolescent is looked down on because he does not work and American culture values competition, productivity, and achievement. Without rewards from the occupational system the adolescent attempts to compensate for low regard by over-conforming to the materialistic norms of American culture. "The right to participate in the larger system symbolizes society's acceptance of him as a responsible person" (Lyell, 1973).

As individuals we want as much from life as we can get, according to (Stringer, 1971), and as social beings we feel threatened by the greed and power of every other individual. Rather than seeing it as a power struggle as seen by

---

V. Meyer (1973). The Psychology of the Young Adult. *Nursing Clinics of North America*, 8, 6-7. Reprinted by Permission of W.B. Saunders Company.

R. Lyell (1973). Adolescent and Adult Self-Esteem As Related to Cultural Values. *Adolescence*, 8, 87. Reprinted by Permission of Libra Publisher, Inc.

a ten-year old, we adults see the need to establish a workable balance between what we want to demand of ourselves and what society demands of us. We recognize that just as society is a threat to the individual who seizes too much power for himself, so the individual is a threat to the society that tries to keep him subjugated and powerless. Whether the society we refer to is a nation or state; a classroom or a family, we have begun to understand that it takes strong and healthy individuals to make a strong and healthy society (Stringer, 1971).

Educationally, curriculum at the elementary level should provide recognized opportunities to foster a healthy self-concept in each child, which is basic to developing feelings of worth and dignity as an adult.

From her study of baccalaureate nursing students (Klug, 1989) reported there was little evidence of increased self-concept over the two-year period of upper division study. Student comments at the completion of their program indicated they generally felt positive about themselves, that the nursing program increased their self-confidence; that clinical experience increased their self-esteem; and with increased nursing responsibilities they believed their self-concept would increase (Klug, 1989).

Women and Self-Esteem

Women in a male-dominated world face many obstacles that men do not face. Every gain that women have made toward greater equality in the work place, in professions, in religious institutions, in the media, in the eyes of the law, and in the interpersonal sphere, has been as a result of real struggling on the part of individual women working together. It is only through raising ourselves in our own estimation that we can increase the self-esteem of all women.

A person who has high self-esteem does not vainly consider himself/

herself better than others or as the center of the universe; Neither does the person see himself/ herself valueless or an inconsequential creature. Rather, he/ she knows many aspects of himself/ herself, has self respect, is aware and is appreciative of worth. The individual recognizes that he/ she is not perfect, but rather than dwelling on flaws and mistakes, the individual sees these characteristics as being human (Sanford and Donovan, 1984).

Obstacles to the Growth of Self-Esteem

Some of the examples of obstacles that interfere with the growth of self-esteem include:

From parents . . .

Conveying that the child is not "enough".

Ridiculing or humiliating the child.

Attempting to control the child by shame and guilt.

Over-protecting the child while obstructing normal learning and self-reliance.

Raising a child with no rules with lack of a supporting structure while inhibiting normal growth.

Denying a child's perception of reality during development and encouraging the child to doubt his/her mind.

Terrorizing a child with physical violence or the threat of it, and instilling acute fear as a lasting characteristic at the child's core. Treating a child as a

---

L. Stringer (1971). *The Sense of Self.* Philadelphia: Temple University Press. Reprinted by Permission of Temple University.

L. Sanford and M. Donovan (1984). *Women and Self-Esteem.* Harrisonburg, VA: R.R. Donnelley and Sons, Company. Reprinted by Permission of Bantam Doubleday Dell Publishing Group Inc.

sexual object.

Teaching the child that he/she is bad, unworthy, or sinful by nature (Branden, 1992).

Since self-esteem is a powerful human need, it is an essential contribution to the life processes; it is indispensable to normal and healthy development; it has survival value. When self-esteem is low, the resilience in the face of life's adversities is diminished. Individuals then tend to be influenced by a desire to avoid pain rather than experience joy. Negatives have more power over individuals than positives.

When individuals become addicted to alcohol or drugs and even destructive relationships, the unconscious intention is invariably to ameliorate anxiety and pain. Addicts are *more* fearful rather then *less* fearful than other human beings. The effort should be directed toward developing realistic confidence. Self-esteem empowers, it motivates, and it energizes. At this moment in history, self-esteem has become a supremely important economic need along with a normal psychological need in order to adapt to an increasingly complex, challenging and competitive world. It is a well recognized fact that peer relationships are very important during adolescence for their future adjustment. Adolescents turn from their families to peers as they attempt to attain autonomy and independence. These experiences with their age group help them to become more sensitive to their own needs and the needs of others (Branden, 1992).

One measure used in studying self-perceived, unpopularity used by Cohen et al (1994) was The Piers-Harris Children's Self-Concept Scale

---

N. Branden (1992). *The Power of Self-Esteem*. Deerfield Beach, Florida: Health Communications, Inc. (c) (1992). Reprinted by Permission of Health Communication, Inc.

Popularity Cluster (1984). They found that feelings of unpopularity in middle childhood increased the risk of similar feelings in adolescence. Self-reports of popularity at age nine, however, were not strong predictors of emotional and antisocial problems at age fifteen. There is a need for additional study of self-perceptions at different ages.

In related research, the only problems having a significant impact on unpopularity in adolescence were those rated by adolescents themselves. The mothers' ratings suggest that mothers of adolescents are not fully attuned to their adolescents' inner feelings. When the same group was studied at grade three, however, mothers and teachers were aware of childrens' feelings and they confirmed the emotional discomfort that children actually experienced when they felt unpopular (Cohen et al, 1993).

In rating unpopularity, the different outcomes may have been due to different criteria used. Adult observers and peers may rate on the basis of aggressive behavior, such as fighting that could lead to difficulties with the law and later in life. On the other hand, self-perceived unpopularity may well reflect an internal condition which predicts later emotional discomfort, but not necessarily unacceptable kinds of behavior leading to intervention by authorities (Cohen et al, 1994).

Early Intervention

There is an opportunity for preventive work by social workers. They can encourage teachers to refer youngsters who have unpopular self-perceptions.

E. Cohen, H. Reinherz, and A. Frost (1994). Self-Perceptions of Unpopularity in Adolescence: Links to Past and Current Adjustment. *Child and Adolescent Social Work Journal*, 11, (1), 37-52. Reprinted by Permission of Plenum Publishing Corp. 233 Spring Street, New York, N.Y., 10013.

After referral, appropriate treatment strategies can be implemented, ranging from social skill groups for the individual to family therapy.

During adolescence, group therapy may be a valuable modality. Receiving feedback and support from peers may be beneficial. Support and education groups for parents of unpopular youths and adolescents can provide opportunities for mothers and fathers to share concerns, to learn about stresses and tasks that vulnerable youngsters confront. In this way parents can assist and become advocates for their children (Cohen et al, 1994).

Returning to (Lidz, 1968), man's biological makeup demands that he grow up in a family or reasonable substitute for family, for protection, nurturance during immaturity and also in order to be directed into becoming an integrated person who assimilated the techniques, knowledge, and roles needed for adaptation and survival. He must grow into and internalize the institutions and roles of the social systems and identify with persons who have assimilated the culture. Characteristics are acquired through identification and by reactions to parental objects and through finding reciprocal roles with them. Capacities to acquire verbal tools necessary for collaborative interactions with others, to think and direct the self, depend greatly upon guardianship within the family and upon the parents' styles of communicating (Lidz, 1968).

Allen et al (1994) in their recent study, examined links between processes of establishing autonomy and relatedness in adolescent family interactions and adolescent's psychosocial development. Increases in adolescent's ego

---

Dr. Joseph P. Allen, S. Hauser, K. Bell, and T. O'Connor (1994). Longitudinal Assessment of Autonomy and Relatedness in Adolescent-Family Interactions as Predictors of Adolescent Ego Development and Self-Esteem. *Child Development* 65, 179-194. Reprinted by Permission of *The Society for Research in Child Development Inc.*, Chicago, IL. February 13, 1995.

development and self-esteem over time were predicted by fathers' behaviors challenging adolescents' autonomy and relatedness, and only when these occurred in the context of the fathers' overall display of autonomous relatedness with the adolescent was this true.

REFERENCES

Chapter V

Allen, J., Hauser, S., Bell, K., and O'Connor, T. (1994). Longitudinal Assessment of Autonomy and Relatedness in Adolescent-Family Interactions as Predictors of Adolescent Ego Development and Self-Esteem. *Child Development* 65, 179-194.

Beane, J., Lipka, R., and Ludewig, J. (1980). Research Synthesis on Self-Concept. *Educational Leadership*, 38, 84-89.

Branden, N. (1992). *The Power of Self-Esteem.* Deerfield Beach, FL: Health Communications, Inc.

Cohen, E., Reinherz, H., and Frost, A. (1994). Self-Perceptions of Unpopularity in Adolescence: Links to Past and Current Adjustment. *Child and Adolescent Social Work Journal*, 11, (1), 37-52.

Emmerich, W. (1959). Parental identification in young children. *Genet. Psycho. Monogram.* 60: 257-308.

Kagan, J. (1958). The concept of identification. *Psychological Review*, 65, 296-305.

Klug, C. (1989). Changes in Self-Concept During Baccalaureate Nursing Education. *Nurse Educator*, 14, (2), 7-11.

Lidz, T. (1968). *The Person: His Development throughout the Life Cycle.* New York: Basic Books, Inc., Publishers.

Lyell, R. (1973). Adolescent and Adult Self-Esteem As Related to Cultural Values. *Adolescence*, 8, 87.

Myer, V. (1973). The Psychology of the Young Adult. *Nursing Clinics of North America*, 8, 6-7.

Sanford, L. and Donovan, M. (1984). *Women and Self-Esteem.* Harrisonburg, VA: R.R. Donnelley and Sons, Company.

Sarbin, T. (1954). *Handbook of Social Psychology*, ed. Gardner Lindzey. Cambridge, MA: Addison-Wesley Publishing Co.

Stringer, L. (1971). *The Sense of Self.* Philadelphia: Temple University Press.

Sullivan, H.S. (1947). *Conceptions of Modern Psychiatry.* Washington: Wm. Alanson White Psychiatric Foundation.

Turner, J. and Helms, D. (1979). *Life Span Development.* Philadelphia: W.B. Saunders Co.

CHAPTER VI

STRESS And Effects on Society

Volumes have been written in the past several years about stress and how to prevent excessive stress to stay reasonabily healthy. It seems logical to include this concept as basic to the constructive/destructive cycle of life, and the multiple effects stress can have on the individual person and on groups of people. The topic will be approached with the assumption that the reader will already have some understanding of the concept of stress and may also have been exposed to some research findings in the literature regarding this timely topic.

Selye (1956) described *stress as essentially the rate of all the wear and tear caused by life*. This term was not entirely new in medicine, but its meaning had not been defined before. The eminent physiologist, Walter B. Cannon, introduced the term *homeostasis*, and he spoke in general terms of stress and strains caused when disease puts pressure on certain specific mechanisms necessary for homeostasis, which is, the maintenance of a normal steady state of the body. As Selye noted, scientists are beginning to see that many common diseases are largely due to errors of adaptive responses to stress, rather than

---

Hans Selye (1956). *The Stress of Life*. New York: McGraw-Hill Book Company. Reprinted by Permission of McGraw-Hill.

relating the disease entirely to direct damage by germs, poisons, or other external agents. In this sense many nervous and emotional disturbances, high blood pressure, gastric and duodenal ulcers, certain types of rheumatic, allergic, cardiovascular, and renal diseases are apparently *diseases of adaptation.*

Selye (1956) pondered the questions he had during his early medical education in both classroom and clinical experience. He had an impression that the diffuse joint and muscle pains identified by people, intestinal disturbances with loss of appetite and weight loss, or complaints of just feeling ill, were equivalents of the experimental syndrome (adrenocortical stimulation, thymicolymphatic atrophy, intestinal ulcers) that he had produced with a variety of toxic substances in the rat.

And, believing that was the case, it would mean that some degree of nonspecific damage would be super-imposed upon specific characteristics of any disease and upon specific effects of any drug. Selye felt if it could be proven that the individual organism had a general nonspecific reaction-pattern with which it could meet damage caused by potential disease producers, this defensive response would level itself to an objective, scientific analysis. And, by clearing up the mechanism of response through which nature herself fights injuries of various kinds, we could learn how to improve upon this reaction when it is imperfect. This whole idea caused Selye to return to his earlier study of stress rather than return to classical endocrinology.

The three reactions stages were described as:

1. The *alarm reaction* - the initial response;
2. *Stage of resistance* - the second stage; and
3. *Stage of exhaustion* - the third phase.

The entire non-specific response Selye called the general *adaptation syndrome* (G.A.S.)

The syndrome was called *general* because general effects were caused by agents; The term *adaptive* was used because defense is stimulated which helps acquisition and maintenance of a stage of inurement; and the term *syndrome* described individual manifestations as coordinated and partly dependent upon each other (Selye, 1956).

Life Events and Effects

Life events are considered nonphysical stressors, and data suggest there is a positive relationship between those events and the occurrence of illness subsequently. This is a complex relationship and obviously dependent on a variety of situational, individual, and constitutional differences.

Lief (1948) related that Adolf Meyer was one of the first to recognize and measure the effect of significant daily life occurrences on subsequent illness. He organized the medical, psychological, and sociological data on his life chart for each individual, and from the charts, he noted emergence of patterns. Stressors and illness relationship have been investigated for quite a long time.

Bieliauskas (1982) suggests guidelines to determine the vulnerability of an individual to illness once we know what the person perceives as a stressor. Pertinent questions need to be asked as,

1. Does the patient have enough personal and interpersonal re- sources to cope with the stress?
2. In the past, has he or she had success coping with such stressors?
3. Does the individual (patient) feel (sense) some degree of confidence in his ability to predict and cope with the stress?

L. Bieliauskas (1982). *Stress and Its Relationship to Health and Illness.* Boulder, Colorado: Westview Press. Reprinted by Permission of Author.

86

4. Is the stressor a byproduct of the illness?

5. Is there a past history of the individual's general health?

6. Is the individual (patient) free of other general stressors?

With negative answers to the above questions, their research has indicated an increase in probability that stressing life events will lead to illness for that person.

The male species has been observed more specifically after stress-related experiences than our female population, particularly in World War I and II, according to (Lamott, 1975).

Predisposing factors were obviously important in attempting to understand individual response to intense stress such as combat. Civilian experiences of war were also destructive in different ways and in some cases responses were delayed over time.

Lamott (1975) suggested the same stressor could produce a variety of reactions, with each individual responding to stress that may well be determined both by genetic heritage and by the individual's experience in life. Some examples may include the development of an ulcer or high blood pressure; some may experience back pain, headaches, diarrhea, insomnia, or asthmatic symptoms, while others may develop arthritis or rheumatism. Volumes have been published from research completed relating to specific diseases or illnesses related to stress.

The explosion in communication and technical development has moved more rapidly than previous revolutions in earlier history, which has created a sense of uneasiness in some members of society. Computerization generally in

---

Kenneth Lamott (1975). *Escape From Stress*. New York: G.P. Putnam's Sons. Reprinted by Permission of the Putnam Publishing Group: (c) (1974).

business, in personal communication -- in almost everything we come in contact with -- helps to pressure certain age groups and some of the social strata who are expected to assimilate this progressive means of communicating. It has been discussed by educators and others that the human mind can assimilate change gradually in day-to-day functioning, but it will be stressed by overload or attempting to progress too quickly or too radically. Marked change has been typical the latter half of the twentieth century.

Effects of the Coping Process

Cohen et al (1986) referred to the influential aspects of Selye's model and the argument that there is a cost to the adaptive process. The cost refers to deleterious effects of some encounter with a stressor that occurs as a consequence of the coping process employed (cf Cohen, 1980; DuBos, 1968; Glass & Singer, 1972). They called these *indirect* or *secondary* effects of one's exposure to a stressor which occur because of the coping process rather than from the stressor itself. This theory suggests that the process of active coping can have a severe impact on one's health and behavior, whether the process was successful or not. In some situations the impact is mediated by physiological processes, while in other cases it is mediated by behavioral processes. The deleterious effects that may occur when,

(a) An individual engages in effortless coping,

(b) An individual persists in using a certain coping response in situations where the response or strategy is not adaptive,

(c) The coping responses have deleterious effects, and

S. Cohen, G. Evans, D. Stokols, and D. Krantz (1986). *Behavior, Health and Environmental Stress*. New York: Plenum Press. Reprinted by Permission of Plenum Publishing Corp., 233 Spring Street, New York, N.Y. 10013.

88

(d) The individual perceives that his/her efforts to cope are fruitless.

There are no definite conclusions available on passivity of the individual in the presence of a stressor.

Coping With Stress

Stress may be a destructive element in people's lives, but the way one reacts to the stress is probably of most importance, so says (Siegel, 1986). Hans Selye is described as a shining example of an accepting attitude relating to his development of reticulum cell sarcoma at age 65 years of age. His understanding of the low cure rate of this type cancer led him to prepare for death initially, but realized he could take one of two approaches during this stress period. He could go around like a miserable candidate on death row and whimper away a year or whatever, or he could try to squeeze as much from life possible, so he chose the latter, as a fighter, and later stated that cancer had provided him with the biggest fight of his life. He accepted this as a natural experience and after a year, two, and three years, he found he was a fortunate exception. Later, Selye consciously cut down on his stress level. At that particular time he was unsure of the relationship between stress and cancer, but he believed as a scientist that the majority of physical illnesses have in part some psychosomatic origin. Siegel (1986) believes Dr. Selye was overly cautious about this relationship and he believes in particular, the onset and course of disease are strongly linked to a person's ability and his or her willingness to cope with stress. Siegel further suggests that the stresses we choose evoke a totally different response from those we would like to avoid and cannot avoid. "Helplessness, he stated, is worse than the stress itself".

B. Siegel (1986). *Love, Medicine & Miracles*. New York: Harper and Row, Publishers. (c) (1986). Reprinted by permission of Harper Collins Publishers.

The level of stress is determined partly by society. Cultures that place the highest value on the individualism and competition combination are the most stressful. On the other hand, the close-knit communities in which there is a supportive, loving relationship as the norm, with the elderly retaining an active role, seem to produce the least stress and have the lowest rates of cancer. Also, religious faith and a fairly open, accepting attitude toward sexuality are two common characteristics of low cancer societies (Siegel, 1986).

In seeking the source of stressors in the structure of experiences rather than life events that are unrelated, (Whelan, 1993) has drawn on theoretical literature relating to conceptualization of poverty to develop a measure of deprivation which provides a reasonable indicator of chronic stress. The major influence of psychological distress is exposure to chronic economic stress. Enforced deprivation of socially defined necessities has a real impact on emotional well-being, although instrumental and emotional support are available. Nonetheless, social support does play an important buffering role, but is not a panacea (Whelan,1993).

Christopher T. Whelen (1993). The role of social support in mediating the psychological consequences of economic stress. *Sociology of Health and Illness.* 15 (1) pp. 86-101. Reprinted by Permission of Blackwell Publishers. ISSN 0141-9889.

REFERENCES

Bieliauskas, L.A. (1982). STRESS AND ITS RELATIONSHIP TO HEALTH AND ILLNESS. Boulder, Colorado: Westview Press.

Cohen, S., Evans, G., Stokols, D., and Krantz, D. *Behavior, Health, and Environmental Stress*. New York: Plenum Press.

Lamott, K. (1975). *Escape From STRESS*. New York: G.P. Putnam's Sons.

Lief, A. (ed) (1948). *The common-sense psychiatry of Dr. Adolf Meyer*. New York: McGraw-Hill Co.

Selye, H. (1956). *The Stress of Life*. New York: McGraw-Hill Book Company.

Siegel, B. (1986). *Love, Medicine & Miracles*. New York: Harper and Row, Publishers.

Whelan, Christopher, T. (1993). The role of social support in mediating the psychological consequences of economic stress. *Sociology of Health and Illness*. 15 (1) ISSN 0141-9889, pp. 86-101.

CHAPTER VII

Crisis Theory Development

The Impact of Change

Changes in a community or in government frequently result from the ideology of one person, one family, or a small group of people having had a unique experience. One such example is that of the late President John Kennedy, who had a sister who was somewhat retarded and later she was institutionalized, which may have had some relationship to President Kennedy's message on Mental Illness and Mental Retardation to the United States Congress on February 5, 1963. He *heralded* the beginning of a revolution in American psychiatry. He said: 'I propose a national mental health program to assist in the inauguration of a wholly new emphasis and approach to care for the mentally ill . . . . Governments at every level -- Federal, State, and Local -- private foundations and individual citizens must all face up to their responsibilities in this area' (Kennedy, 1963, p. 2).

It was noted by President Kennedy that although the care of our mentally ill in the United States was equivalent or perhaps better than care in many countries, it was obvious that some hospitals and homes were unpleasant institutions that were shamefully understaffed.

Prior to this time, there had been increasing interest of the state and federal legislators in the community problem presented by the needed care of mentally ill and the mentally retarded persons in light of the large numbers, the social disorganization and suffering cause, along with the drain on community resources. One consequence of this interest was the Mental Health Study Act of 1955, whereby Congress directed the establishment of a Joint Commission on Mental Illness and Health. The legislators were primarily oriented to preventive programs. With the impressive membership and supporters in the study of the mental health needs and resources of this country as a foundation, the report of the Joint Commission provided a competent survey of the mental health field. The national and state legislators advocated comprehensive, preventive and a community approach, while the mental health professionals were more restricted to the adult mentally ill without emphasis on the mentally retarded or for children suffering from mental disorders. They further focused on improving the mental hospitals through reducing their size, improving resources and extending services into the community, dealing with acute and chronic psychotic patients that were obviously neglected.

President Kennedy's message following the Joint Commission of 1961, emphasized a new mental health program with comprehensive community care. He maintained that the need was to return mental health care to the mainstream of American medicine, and at the same time upgrade mental health services. Despite some disappointment, these psychiatrists derived definite satisfaction from terms of the President's message. The Community Mental Health Centers Act of 1963 was designed to set up a country-wide system of community mental health centers, to provide services for prevention or diagnosis of mental illness; care and treatment of mentally ill patients, or rehabilitation of such persons (U.S.

House of Representatives, 1963, p.19).

Definition of 'Preventive Psychiatry'

For Caplan (1964), 'preventive psychiatry' refers to the body of theoretical and practical professional knowledge which may be utilized to plan and carry out programs for reducing,

(1)   the incidence of mental disorders of all types in the community, which is ('primary prevention'),

(2)   the duration of a significant number of those disorders which do occur ('secondary prevention'), and

(3)   the impairment which may result from those disorders 'tertiary prevention').

It was anticipated that the psychiatrist had developed a close working relationship through clinical practice with psychologists, psychiatric social workers, and nurses, therefore, he/she must be extended in preventive psychiatry to include collaboration with social scientists, economists, legislators, citizen leaders, along with professional workers in public health, welfare, religious and educational fields.

Life Crises

It is essential to remember the significance of personality development (Chapter 2), before attempting to understand why life events can be natural happenings for some, but may well serve as a basis for crisis in other individuals.

Psychosocial supplies normally include stimulation of an individual's

---

Gerald Caplan (1964). *Principles of Preventive Psychiatry.* New York: Basic Books Inc., Publishers.   Copyright (c) (1970).   Reprinted by Permission of Basic Books, Inc., a Division of Harper Collins Publishers, Inc.

cognitive and affective development, resulting through personal interaction with others who are significant in the family, with peers, and with older people in school, church, and work. In considering needs, they can be placed in three areas, one of needs for exchange of love and affection, another of the need for limitation and control (considering assertion patterns and submission to authority), and a third of needs for participation in activity with others, in relation to the degree of support or independence in dealing with a task.

In line with the values of a culture, a "healthy" relationship is one in which the significant other person perceives, respects, and attempts to satisfy needs of the person in a manner which conforms to their respective social role. Expectations by others of a person's behavior profoundly influences actions and feelings about the self. As they arrange a place in the structure of the individual's society, they prescribe a place in life for that individual to a degree. Inner strength is supplemented with rewards and external security from that position. So, one could say, if a person is born into an advantaged group in a stable society, there is a probability that this individual's social roles and their expected changes over a lifetime will provide adequate opportunities for healthy personality development. On the other hand, if the individual belongs to a disadvantaged group or an unstable society, the progress may be blocked for him or her, who may also be deprived of challenge and opportunity, which may well affect the mental health of the person negatively.

In addition to behavioral prescriptions which influence role relations with others in the environment, the group culture, including language, values, and traditions, will have a major influence on the way he or she perceives reality along with the attitudes and aspirations of this individual. It would follow, the richer the cultural heritage of this individual, the more likely the person will have been taught to handle more complicated problems. The more stable the society, the more likely that there were provisions for acquiring perception tools, problem-solving skills, and values to guide the person in dealing with life's difficulties. Although somewhat arbitrary, conditions of mental health are categorized as physical, psychosocial, and socio-cultural supplies, which are all interwoven inextricably in life. And, besides, the individual is not simply a passive recipient of these supplies and a passive victim when there is a deficient quality or quantity. Rather, he or she modifies his physical and psychosocial environment significantly, from the earliest years, and then as a member of social and political groups the individual may also influence his/her socio-cultural supplies (Caplan, 1964).

The Significance of Life Crises

For some the concept of crisis is a negative event in one's life experience. From observations of individual life experiences over time, it has been determined that some stages of crisis can serve as a growth opportunity -- a period of learning healthy adaptation. With adequate problem-solving skills, the person who has experienced a crisis event and adapted adequately to the situation, hopefully will return to the pre-crisis state. In addition, there is the potential for learning new and additional skills in dealing with a crisis event that could help to prepare the person more appropriately for a future crisis.

Caplan (1964) in examining histories of psychiatric patients during crisis periods, the individual seems to have dealt with problems in a maladaptive way, and evolved less healthy coping skills than before the crisis. In these cases, the progression toward eventual mental illness appears to have accelerated during successive crisis situations. Or other patients, who eventually became ill, their downward path seems to have been delayed periodically by a successful adjustive experience during a crisis event. Novelists and dramatists have exemplified the popular views on crisis as a turning point in life development.

98

Erich Lindemann (1944) who studied bereavement reactions among survivors of those killed in the Coconut Grove night club fire in Boston, developed fundamentals of Crisis Theory as a conceptual framework for preventive Psychiatry. He made an important contribution to the field of crisis. (See Chapter 8, Loss, Grief and Grieving).

Characteristics of Crisis

The occurrence of crisis is an imbalance between the difficulty and importance of the problem and resources immediately available to deal with it. The direct problem-solving mechanisms that create the usual homeostasis do not work. Tension due to frustration of need rises which is threatening to maintaining integrity of the organism or group and may be associated with feelings of subjective discomfort or displeasure called an upset, such as anxiety, fear, guilt, shame, and even a feeling of helplessness.

Caplan (1964) described the four phases,

Phase 1.   Initial rise in tension from stimulus impact calling forth the habitual problem-solving responses of homeostasis;

Phase 2.   Lack of success and continued stimulus is associated with rise in tension;

Phase 3.   As tension rises to the third threshold it acts as a powerful internal stimulus to mobilize internal and external resources. Through trial-and-error in action or abstract thought, redefinition of the problem may evolve and it is possible for resolution of the problem or upset, at this phase;

Phase 4.   If the problem can neither be solved with need satisfaction nor avoided by need resignation or perceptual distortion, the problem continues and tension mounts to a threshold over time to a breaking point. This phase involves major disorganization of the individual and sometimes the occurrence of drastic results.

The resolution of crisis is significant in relation to the individual's future mental health. The new equilibrium may be better or worse than previously. New socially acceptable, problem-solving techniques may be developed as a healthy outcome. On the other hand, new coping responses that are socially unacceptable may be utilized dealing with difficulties by evasion, irrational fantasy manipulation, or regression and alienation, which may increase the likelihood of dealing maladaptively with future difficulties. The new coping pattern may well become an integral part of the individual's problem-solving responses to future hazards (Caplan, 1964).

Some Regularities in Crisis

According to Hansell (1976),

1. *The individual* shows a narrowed, a fixed span of attention.
2. *The individual* shows some 'loosening' and 'widening' of affectional attachments.
3. *The individual-in-distress* experiences a profound loss of attachment to a clear vision of his/her identity.
4. *The individual-in-distress* usually shows socially unsatis-factory performance of his/her roles.
5. *The individual-in-distress* experiences an altered state of consciousness, including a random-access memory.
6. *The individual-in-distress* experiences a markedly reduced ability to make decisions.
7. *The individual-in-distress* sends signals of distress.

In summary, there are characteristic alterations of attention, identity, affectional attachments, memory, role performance, decision-making and distress signalling which combine to create a biologically flexible, transition state.

Essential Attachments

Hansell (1976) identified seven essential attachments. Each of the seven categories of necessary transaction with the environment is considered separately, essential. Together as a set, they are a relatively complete account of all connections. Each is necessary for a person's survival; when the seven are intact, they are sufficient for survival. The categories of attachment are interdependent. So if one kind of attachment is severed and remains so for more than a brief period, the damage spreads to other kinds of attachments. Each attachment is like the need for oxygen, upon which life depends. The organism needs oxygen even if it has abundant supplies of water and food.

The seven essential attachments are as follows:

1. To: *Food, oxygen*, and information of requisite variety: biochemical and informational supplies;

2. To: A clear concept of a *self-identity*, held with conviction;

3. To: Persons, at lease one, in persisting, *inter-dependent contact*, occasionally approximating intimacy;

4. To: *Groups*, at lease one, comprised of individuals who regard this person as a member;

5. To: *Roles*, at least one, which offer a context for achieving *dignity*, and *self-esteem*, through performance;

Norris Hansell (1976). *The Person-In-Distress*. New York: Human Sciences Press. (c) (1976). Published by Permission of Human Sciences Press, Inc., - Plenum Publishing Corp.

6.   To: *Money*, or purchasing power, to participate in an exchange of goods and services in a society specialized for such exchanges;

7.   To: A comprehensive *system of meaning*, a satisfying set of notions which clarify experience and define ambiguous events. *Necessity*, means that a person, or the personality, atrophies if any attachment is severed.

Sufficiency means, as a set, the seven attachments include all the lines of behavior known to maintain a vital exchange with the environment.

In summary, perspectives which describe the ordinary social attachments of human beings can give direction to assist the distressed person to conduct their work of adaptation.   For the helpers, the concept of 'seven essential attachments' are designated to direct their attention toward 'the larger picture', as they assess a troubled individual's current situation (Hansell, 1976).

Impact of Stress on Older Adults

At present we are a society weighted heavily with older adults, and with increased longevity, this will become more problematic with stress and crisis experiences.   There is naturally a greater potential for illness with increasing age, along with fewer actual supports or resources among family and friends, and the majority of these older adults will have experienced losses.   The loss of identity through retirement or a job loss can be a common occurrence and many will have lost loved ones to death, and will be dealing with the process of bereavement.

There are personnel prepared at various levels from a Psychiatric Aide to a Psychiatrist, but many members of our populace are resistant to seeking help from a professional with mental health expertise.   Although people are educated to recognize irregular symptoms in themselves and others and are encouraged to seek help early as a preventive measure, the recommendations are apparently not strong enough to offset the stigma or concept of mental health care. With the realization of physical care needs and mental health care needs so closely interrelated, it is difficult to determine clearcut symptomatology.

Phillips and Murrell (1994) studied special populations of adults 55 and over, over a two-year period, to determine the impact of potential stressors like physical health, stressful events, and social support, as to their seeking mental health care. The control group of nonseekers of help was compared to those who sought help that could be considered for mental health care needs.

The researchers included variables particularly relevant to experiences in later life which may uniquely contribute to mental health needs of aged individuals. By using a prospective design, measures were obtained six months prior to the point in which the mental health need was reported, and the researchers were able to obtain an accurate assessment of the psychological, social, physical, and environmental conditions that existed before professional help was sought.

For whatever reason, help seekers almost unanimously sought services of a medical doctor for help with their emotional problems. The help seekers experienced higher levels of unpleasant events prior and during the time when help was sought, compared with nonseekers. As hypothesized, events involving bereavement, social and economic loss, and physical illness were far more common among help seekers than nonseekers. The social network may have been restricted more so as a consequence of the losses which may have demanded greater reliance on professional helpers (Phillips and Murrell (1994).

Specialized mental health programs for the geriatric population have been

---

M.A. Phillips & S.A. Murrell (1994). Impact of Psychological and Physical Health, Stressful Events, and Social Support on Subsequent Mental Health Help Seeking Among Older Adults. *Journal of Consulting and Clinical Psychology*, 62, (2). 270-275. Reprinted by Permission of American Psychological Association.

found to be effective and used frequently, (Light, Lebowitz, and Bailey, 1986; Rosen, Coppage, Troglin, & Rosen, 1981), demonstrating that efforts to provide special care to older adults can yield positive results. The present study suggests that mental health care specialists are under-represented among providers of care to the older population. There needs to be a special effort made to develop and implement the kinds of services that would encourage increased use among older adults.

E. Light, B.D. Lebowitz, and F. Bailey (1986). CMHC's and elderly services: An analysis of direct and indirect services and service delivery sites. *Community Mental Health Journal*, 22, 294-302. Reprinted by Permission of Plenum Publishing Corp.

REFERENCES

Caplan, G. (1964). *Principles of Preventive Psychiatry*. New York: Basic Books Inc., Publishers.

Hansell, N. (1976). *The Person-In-Distress*. New York: Human Sciences Press.

Kennedy, J.F. 'Message from the President of the United States Relative to Mental Illness and Mental Retardation', February 5, 1963, 88th. Congress, First Session, House of Representatives, Document No. 58.

Light, E., Lebowitz, B.D. & Bailey, F. (1986). CMHC's and elderly services: An analysis of direct and indirect services and service delivery sites. *Community Mental Health Journal*, 22, 294-302.

Phillips, M.A. & Murrell, S.A. (1994). Impact of Psychological and Physical Health, Stressful Events, and Social Support on Subsequent Mental Health Help Seeking Among Older Adults. *Journal of Consulting and Clinical Psychology*, 62, (2), 270-275.

United States House of Representatives #3688, 88th. Congress, First Session, 1963. A bill to provide for assistance in the construction and initial operation of community mental health centers and for other purposes.

CHAPTER VIII

Loss, Grief and Grieving

Loss As A Type of Crisis

During the period of crisis related to a loss, a rather minor force acting for a relatively short period of time can help to bring the balance of mental health to the client, or person involved.

It was proposed by both Dr. Lindemann and Dr. Caplan (1963) that from primitive time on, every religion has recognized that people must be helped to mourn and to express their grief. Every modern religion has a ritual for death and burial, time set aside for condolence, and a way for family and friends to congregate and talk about the person who is gone — a time for mourning and remembering together.

Although the essential work of mourning and work surmounting a crisis must be done by the person who is deeply involved in the loss, the individual needs real help from people around him or her, if this person is to emerge and proceed in a healthy fashion.

The Harvard Study recommended *a way in which all of us can help those we love to face a crisis*, with the belief that during a crisis period, a little help

G. Caplan (1963). *Principles of Preventive Psychiatry*. New York: Basic Books, Publishers. Reprinted by Permission of Basic Books, a Division of Harper Collins Publishers, Inc.

goes a long way. They further suggested the helping hand that will no doubt make a difference:

1. *Help confront the crisis.*
2. *Help confront the crisis - in manageable doses.*
3. *Help to find the facts.*
4. *Don't give false reassurance.*
5. *Don't encourage to blame others.*
6. *Help the individual to accept help.*
7. *Help with the everyday tasks.*(Caplan, 1963)

Parental Death

It is well known that children are protected from death whenever possible in our society. There are some exceptions in families who take the child at any age to the mortuary or to funeral services, and generalize their explanations of death to the child. Usually the child learns about death of animals or pets before they are exposed to death of a person, unless a parent, sibling, or grandparent dies early in the child's life experience. The pet loss experience is authentic and helpful if the child is helped to endure the loss through the feeling of sorrow, and assisting in the burial ritual in a special way.

Gardner (1990) believes the child should be invited to attend both services and burial of a parent. Children seem to learn best from mastery of concrete experiences. Although a funeral can be morbid it can provide such an

---

R.A. Gardner (1990). Object Loss Due to Death of Parent of Sibling in *Stressors and the Adjustment Disorders.* (Ed.) Noshpitz, J.D. and Coddington, R.D. New York: John Wiley & Sons — A Wiley Interscience publication, pp. 43-44. Reprinted by Permission of John Wiley & Sons and by Author, Richard Gardner, M.D.

experience effectively. The child also has the opportunity to observe the expression of emotion which usually occurs at a funeral, and this will facilitate the child's own emotional expression, which is vital to the healthy process of mourning.

The Mourning Process in Children

The process of mourning is a series of psychological responses that an individual utilizes in the attempt to deal with the death of a meaningful person, according to Gardner (1990). There is general agreement among theorists that in order for children to mourn they must be able to differentiate themselves from the dead person. Anna Freud (1952) held that the capacity for differentiation takes place during the second half of their first year of life. Sigmund Freud (1917/1953) believed that for mourning to take place, the child must first accept that the loved one no longer exists. And without this realization the child cannot withdraw libidinal energy from the lost person and invest it in others. Developmental factors as well as environmental factors play a part in determining when and whether a child can mourn. If children are reared in homes where they have been protected from exposure to death, they are less likely to realize its impact.

There are varied opinions regarding the age at which children exhibit the capacity to mourn because not all environmental factors are taken into consideration. It is suggested that to realize the full significance of death the child goes through a two-stage process. The first stage involves the child's realization that death can occur to others; the second realization that he or she will ultimately suffer this same fate. There may be months or years between the two phases of recognition (Gardner, 1990).

Facilitation of Healthy Mourning

If children are preoccupied with fears that they might die or are unsure of safety and provision for their needs, it would not be possible for the child to mourn effectively. There needs to be some reassurance by the parent or therapists that they will be cared for, and their eminent death is unlikely.

In attempting to explain one's own position regarding the death of the person, some parents give long theological and philosophical explanations, while avoiding direct discussion of the painful reality. This may engender distrust and confusion. Parents should tell the child exactly what his/her view is regarding afterlife, even if they relate they do not know. The parent's bona fide belief may well provide some reassurance to the child (Gardner, 1990).

Substitute Relationship

The mourning process is especially to free the individual from the loved one and to form attachments with others, as a facilitation in continuing meaningful living. Children may need help with this goal. Memories of the lost parent may serve the child well at the time of death and thereafter. Particularly memories of the parent's affection are helpful and reassuring to the child's feeling of self-worth. The advice and teaching of the deceased parent may remain throughout his or her life and contribute to a healthy superego development. The parent's healthy personality traits continue to be incorporated into the psychic structure of the child, which supports a healthy developmental pattern. The most desirable outcome for the mourning child is development of meaningful relationships with substitutes, and the child needs reassurance that it is normal to feel a little guilty as this relationship develops (Gardner, 1990).

Sibling Death

Although the psychological trauma following the death of a sibling is not usually as severe as from the death of a parent, there is a formidable stress and should be addressed in the psychiatric literature in some detail. Again, this experience needs to be considered as an individual experience to be placed in proper perspective.

If the dying sibling is a child and that child is aware of his or her impending death, the siblings can be informed and this provides an opportunity for anticipatory mourning. This improves the capacity for dealing optimally with the sibling's death. Painful subjects that are openly discussed produce less anxiety and less distortions in those involved in the loss. Discussion with healthy siblings relating to an impending death of a sibling should take place in the family context, both with and without the dying child. In a tragic situation, shared grieving can be a cohesive force for the family members.

In addressing the possibility of guilt, it is noted that a variety of factors in sibling death situations cause guilt related to hostility. At times all children feel rivalry with possible hateful feelings toward their siblings. Because of harboring occasional death wishes, the surviving children may feel particularly guilty when a sibling dies. Sometimes well siblings are restricted in their activities because of the terminally ill child and they may wish that the child were already dead. The well child may also be angry at the dying sibling because of the extra attention the sick child is receiving (Gardner, 1990).

In Chapter seven, reference was made to the beginning establishment of

---

Erich Lindemann (1994). Symptomatology and Management of Acute Grief. *American Journal of Psychiatry*, 101, 141-148. Reprinted by Permission of *The American Journal of Psychiatry.*

crisis theory based on Lindemann's study of bereaved disaster victims of the Coconut Grove Fire in Boston, along with other patients who experienced loss. His research findings have been especially helpful in identifying some typical reactions to loss, anticipatory features — less typical reactions, and the development of affective management of grief reactions (Lindemann, 1944).

The observation and sample was comprised of 101 patients — psychoneurotic patients who lost a relative during the course of their treatment; relatives of patients who died in the hospital; bereaved disaster victims (Coconut Grove Fire) and their close relatives; and relatives of members of the armed forces, since this study of psychiatric interviews primarily was completed during wartime. Laboratory and metabolic studies were reported separately in another report. This portion of the report was based only on psychological observations.

Some common points were recognized as follows:

1. Acute grief is a definite syndrome with psychological and somatic symptomatology.

2. This syndrome may happen immediately after a crisis; it sometimes is delayed; it can be exaggerated or apparently absent.

3. Distorted pictures may appear, each of which represents one special aspect of the grief syndrome rather than the typical syndrome.

4. These distorted pictures can be successfully transformed into a normal grief reaction and can be resolved by appropriate techniques. Some of the striking features of persons in acute grief included,

    (1) A marked tendency to sighing respiration, particularly when discussing the grief;

    (2) A complaint about feeling exhausted and lacking strength for normal activities;

(3)   Digestive symptoms such as no appetite, lack of saliva and
      hollow sensation in the stomach.

Generally there was a slight sense of unreality experienced, an emotional distancing from others, and an intense preoccupation with the image of the deceased. There was frequently a strong preoccupation with feelings of guilt, going back to before the death and accusing the self of negligence. In addition, there was often a loss of warmth in relationships with other people; at times the response was in an angry or irritable manner. The speech was frequently pressured in talking of the deceased, along with feelings of restlessness, moving about aimlessly, and the individual had an inability to sit still. There was a lack of initiative or ability to maintain organized patterns of activity. There was a strong dependency on anyone who would stimulate the bereaved to activity and serve as an initiating agent.

There were five major points to be made that seem characteristic and apparently pathognomonic for grief:

(1) Somatic distress,

(2) Preoccupation with the image of the deceased,

(3) Guilt,

(4) Hostile reactions, and

(5) Loss in patterns of conduct.

Patients who border on pathological reactions may behave as the deceased during the last illness. For example, a bereaved man may find himself walking in the manner of his deceased father.

Course of Normal Grief Reactions

This duration of grief reaction seemed to be related to the success with which a person did the *grief work*, or accomplished the emancipation from the bondage of the deceased; readjusted to the environment in which the deceased was missing, and the formulation of new relationships.

Morbid Grief Reactions

Distortions of normal grief were considered morbid grief reactions. The most frequent and striking examples were the *delay* or *postponement* of resolution.

In regards to a *delay* of resolution, if bereavement occurred when the patient was confronted with important tasks and when it seemed necessary to maintain the morale of others, he or she showed little or no reaction for weeks or in some cases much longer.

In regards to a *distorted reaction*, which frequently occurred after a delayed reaction, in the following forms:

(1)   *overactivity without a sense of loss*, rather than a sense of well being;

(2)   *the acquisition of symptoms belonging to the last illness of the deceased*;

(3)   *a recognized medical disease*, one of the psychosomatic conditions. Predominantly these conditions included   ulcerative colitis, rheumatoid arthritis, and asthma;

(4)   *alteration in relationship to friends and relatives*;

(5)   *furious hostility against specific persons*;

(6)   Hidden hostility with wooden and formal affectivity *resembling schizophrenic pictures*;

(7)   Related to the picture was a *lasting loss of patterns of social interaction.*

(8)   If active, the patient's activities became *detrimental to his/her own social and economic existence.* (Loss of friends, status and money are usual results).

(9)   Development of an *agitated depression* with tension, agitation, insomnia, feelings of worthlessness, bitter self-accusation,   and obvious need for punishment — such patients may be dangerously suicidal.

Management

The essential task for the psychiatrist is of sharing the patient's grief work, that is, extricating him/herself from bondage to the deceased and finding new patterns of rewarding interaction. Under-reaction and over-reaction of the bereaved must be given attention.

Religious agencies have provided rituals to help maintain the patient's interaction with others and to help counteract the morbid guilt feelings. Comfort alone, does not assist the patient's grief work adequately. There must be the acceptance of the pain of bereavement. Relationship with the deceased must be reviewed to become acquainted with alterations in his/her own emotional reaction. Then there is a need to express sorrow and sense of loss and to find an acceptable formulation of the future relationship to the deceased. Ultimately, new patterns of conduct will be acquired.

It is suggested that Clergy and non-professional caregivers need to assess symptoms and refer for professional help when indicated (Lindemann, 1944).

Childhood Stress Due to Parental Divorce

One of the obvious stresses created by the divorce is the absence of a parent from the home. The identification process is generally interfered with. Some children view the absent parent as the "abandoner". As a result, a feeling

116

of distrust in that parent may evolve, and that feeling could extend throughout the life span.

When children are involved in the parental conflicts to some degree, there is a greater chance the children will develop some psychological disturbances. The greater capacity the parent has for communication and cooperation the less likely that children will develop real psychological disturbances. The more attentive, involved, and reliable, the absent parent is the lower the probability that children will suffer the stresses that bring about maladaptive adjustment reactions.

The telling children about an anticipated separation is an important part of the plan, which should take place three or four weeks prior to the separation to give children an opportunity to work through this reality. Both parents should do the telling and both have ongoing communication after the initial discussion. Parents need to be honest in their reason for separation, and this prevents the need for children to turn to others for further explanation and provides alternative thinking to children that it is not their fault that this separation is taking place (Gardner, 1990).

To Grieve and to Mourn

There is a definite need for both adults and children to grieve, realizing that attachments are generally formed at all ages, which provide some meaning to life. Understanding there is pleasure and meaning attached to a relationship, we naturally experience pain when separation occurs for whatever reason.

As we reflect on events that occur as an outgrowth of a typical family relationship networking, we realize there are usually separations and losses happening as each member of a family moves gradually through the stages of life. As a person experiences the changes that evolve throughout the life cycle there seems to be an evolving capacity to learn how to mourn or deal with loss. Some theorists believe that the capacity to mourn may not be fully realized until adolescence, and for some it may not be possible until adulthood. At any rate, there is agreement by the majority of professional caregivers that loss does require an individual to grieve and mourn.

At times in clinical practice, it is possible to observe what is considered a delayed reaction to an actual loss, especially considering death as the loss. There may be no overt signs of grief by the person observed at the time of loss but at some later time this same individual may react with extreme grief to a loss of apparent less significance.

In case of a distorted grief reaction, as noted earlier by Lindemann, the bereaved may show minimal signs of grief at the time of loss, but later may develop psychosomatic symptoms as migraines, sensations of dizziness or other symptoms. Anger and irritability are frequently involved which help to lead to conflicts and on to inability to deal with the grief.

Some constructive and healthy activities of the mourning process involve accepting the reality of a specific loss; participating in the burial rites; expressing ones feelings in words to a trusted person; recognizing the intense feelings of desertion felt by the bereaved; resolving the positive and negative feelings toward the lost love object; detaching in a healthy manner, and adopting new hopes and dreams for future orientation.

Guidance and direction can be helpful in renewing social contacts. Counseling is often indicated, which is designed to help the bereaved person mourn their loss more fully and hopefully to prevent subsequent psychopathology. The utilization of an individual's resources can be especially helpful for the bereaved in building independency.

Mourners can be helped to resolve their feeling of loss by demonstrating respect and honor for the loved one. One way in which mourners frequently demonstrate their caring for the deceased person is through the presentation of a Memorial Service.

Stages of Grief

Through reading or lectures, many people in today's society have accepted the important data of Kubler-Ross (1969), as she described the Stages of Death and Dying, after dealing with many terminally ill, dying patients.

First Stage: **Denial and Isolation**

Denial functions as a buffer in case of shocking news, and it permits the patient to collect himself and mobilize appropriate defense, usually less radical than otherwise.

Second Stage: **Anger**

As denial is no longer completely alleviating and satisfactory to the patient, it is replaced by feelings of anger, rage, envy, and resentment. There is a tendency to displace the anger and project it to whomever is available as a target at the moment. For the caregiver, it demands patience and fortitude to remain a therapeutic agent.

Third Stage: **Bargaining**

This is less well known but it is helpful to the patient--for brief periods of time. After the anger, there is a thought of postponing the inevitable death, with kinder words to God for a personal consideration. The wish is for an extension of life.

Fourth Stage: **Depression**

When the terminally ill patient can no longer deny his illness, either by additional treatment or surgery, the feeling of great loss will soon be experienced replacing the anger and rage. The depression seems obvious partially alleviating any shame or guilt the person experiences based on an inability to function in his/her regular role. This is one type depression which takes into account impending losses. An initial reaction many people have is an urge to cheer people up at this stage. But this depression serves as a tool to prepare the ill person for the impending loss of all love objects. It would be contraindicated to tell this person not to be sad, but rather it is helpful to provide an opportunity for the person to express sorrow. This makes the final acceptance easier for the dying patient.

Fifth Stage: **Acceptance**

If there has been sufficient time given to work through the previous stages, the person reaches a stage during which he neither is depressed nor angry about his fate. Having mourned the impending loss, he/she will contemplate the coming end with a rather quiet expectation. While the dying patient has found some peace and acceptance, there may be a time for less visiting; however, having a close relative or friend available may confirm to the dying person that someone will be around until the end. There should be that verbal assurance that someone will be there, perhaps only quietly present (Kubler-Ross, 1969).

Death Education and Research

Formal courses, seminars, or curriculum units on death and dying in schools and colleges have been reviewed as to effectiveness for those involved in the learning activity.

Warren (1989) reported that there was some evidence of increased fear of death for some students after completing a specific course in death and dying,

---

W.G. Warren (1989). *Death Education and Research*. New York: The Haworth Press. Reprinted by Permission of the Haworth Press, Inc.

rather than less, as was predicted. Others suggested no real obvious change after completing a course like this.

Lester, Getty and Kneisl (1974) in an early study of attitudes toward death among nursing personnel, found that increased professional education was associated with decreased fear of death (Warren, 1989).

It would seem there needs to be additional inquiry and perhaps new approaches to study the effects of professional instruction relating to the dying process.

REFERENCES

Caplan, G. (1963). *Principles of Preventive Psychiatry*. New York: Basic Books, Publishers.

Gardner, R.A. (1990). Object Loss Due to Death of Parent or Sibling in *Stressors and the Adjustment Disorders*. (Ed.) *Noshpitz, J.D. and Coddington, R.D.* New York: A Wiley Interscience Publication (John Wiley & Sons), pp. 43-44.

Kubler-Ross, E. (1969). *On Death and Dying*. New York: Macmillan Publishing Company, Inc.

Warren, W.G. (1989). *Death Education and Research*. New York: The Haworth Press.

SUGGESTED READING

Crenshaw, D.A. (1990). *BEREAVEMENT* — Counseling the Grieving throughout the Life Cycle. New York: Crossroad Publishing Co./Herder and Herder.

PART III

DESTRUCTIVE BEHAVIOR

CHAPTER IX

Alcohol and Addictions to Other Drugs

Alcoholism in our American Society

Every human society as known has used alcohol. Each and every society regulates use of alcohol for religious, political, family, and personal purposes. According to Denzin (1987), the American society is a drinking society and it is considered as a right of every American adult to drink. Alcohol is used as a social lubricant; Alcohol is used to celebrate personal and national holidays. Some drink to escape pressures of daily living and to find freedom that daily routines do not allow. Americans associate drinking with thrill seeking, with sports, adventure, and with vacations. It can be said that drinking is basic to the American way of life; however, according to (Denzin, 1987), Americans have problems with alcohol.

An *alcoholic* will be defined as a person who

(1) defines himself/herself as an alcoholic;

(2) has lost the ability to control his or her drinking and one drink sets off a chain of drinking in which the drinker
drinks until intoxicated; and

(3) has an inability to abstain from drinking for any continuous period

of time.

The two basic types of alcoholics are those who continue to drink and those who are recovering.

A *recovering alcoholic* is a once active alcoholic who has stopped drinking. Also, this is one who belongs to a recovery group, often Alcoholics Anonymous (A.A.) (Denzin, 1987).

An Organized Study On Alcohol Prevention

After the report of the National Council on *Alcohol and Public Policy: Beyond the Shadow of Prohibition* published in 1981, the panel, chaired by Mark H. Moore, on the Alternative Policies Affecting the Prevention of Alcohol Abuse and Alcoholism, believed it would amply reward anyone's close attention to share their study. The National Institute on Alcohol Abuse and Alcoholism (NIAAA), who had commissioned the Study, concurred and moved toward organizing a followup conference for 1983 in consideration of recommendations from the findings. The two purposes for conferring were for the generation of wider public knowledge to stimulate responses for researchers and practitioners, and to provide opportunity for learning more about prevention and the integration of voluntary, private, and governmental action, especially local policy initiatives. The panel of thirteen outstanding professionals were representative of Government, Psychiatry, Public Health, Law, Economics, Social Sciences, Medicine, Sociology from the U.S. prestigious Centers and Academia with special competencies.

The three aspects of prevention were,

1. To affect terms under which alcohol is available, special taxes, minimum age requirements, regulation of outlets and availability and times of sale;

2. To shape drinking practices directly by talking with people about safe and appropriate drinking behaviors; and

3. To make for a safer environment in which to drink.

All in all, they believed the nation's strategy should shift toward more kinds of prevention that are oriented approaches to alcohol problems. The content of a few individual panel members will be included as highlighting this section. (Gerstein,(Ed), 1984, pp.1-11).

Helpful Suggestions and Recommendations

In considering the problem of alcohol, youth, and drunk driving, emphasis was placed on parental understanding and what they can do.

According to Keith Schuchard, Parental Resource Institute for Drug Education, we are dealing with an issue that we are hesitant to confront: chemicals that people like, that feel good, that are fun, like alcohol, cocaine, marijuana, and whatever.

It has been difficult and almost impossible for most parents and many health professionals to know what life is like for an ordinary American kid. Children have access to multiple materials in local shopping centers, especially record stores, that glamorize alcohol and cocaine in songs; in T-shirt shops, the display shows increases of drunkenness--oriented T-shirts and multiple designs on shirts with messages encouraging anything except responsible behavior. Examples of drug-oriented comic books are common and they show kids how to shoplift and how to do drugs in the kitchen. Knowing when to take the visine test is obviously one way of keeping your drug participation from your parents.

This representative panel member, K. Schuchard, explains that children are experiencing something no other generation in world history has lived

128

through. The society has forgotten to protect children from commercial manipulation and predatory merchandising. Clever marketing strategies and effective advertising are designed to take advantage of the normal adolescent insecurity.

Some Practical Parental Action

Some parents have begun organizing, educating themselves, and working more effectively with other groups. Many teachers and parents working in the alcohol and drug abuse field are more optimistic about changes observed. One method used to teach parents how to teach their children about alcohol and drugs was to tell them about the biology of pleasure, its meaning, and what can be done to short circuit it. This includes the role that the brain's reward system plays in motivation, desire for achievement, self-discipline, and the like. In an age of physical fitness mania, people are interested in their bodies, especially ages 12 to 14-year olds, whose bodies are probably giving them quite a lot of trouble. Hence, the biological aspects can be an encouraging part of prevention.

One important element in strategy is for parents to network with peer groups, either in an informal or quite an organized way. Parents need to support each other in caring about the health of their children and they need to stick together. It is obviously important for kids to know what their friends are permitted to do. Parents must be made aware of consequences to the misuse of pleasurable chemicals. It is more than just a matter of hitting someone with a car, but of a young person's ability to develop their capacities for controlling impulses in a way that is constructive and can well lead to a productive life (Schuchard, 1984),(pp. 110-136).

Schools and Their Assistance

Sister Madeleine Boyd described Shalom, Inc., the program she developed in Philadelphia for drug and alcohol problems, initially in her school of 3000 girls in Philadelphia's Little Italy. She studied the social patterns of the youth in the area and visited all drug and alcohol programs to see which ones she could use as resources for her students. She concluded that most of the young people in the programs were already scarred and the prevention phase had already passed. She believed it was necessary to teach the youth skills to handle their own problems and to make their own decisions. She made her case sufficiently to get drug and alcohol money mainly because of fear that high school children were becoming involved in criminal behavior. They hired people for the program who had professional life training skills, such as social workers, psychologists, and guidance counselors, who had a way of communicating with teenagers. It was first necessary to gain rapport with the children and learn what they were reading, seeing on television and listening to. Since kids know that alcohol is socially acceptable, sometimes they revert to alcohol use rather than no drug at all to maintain their peer status.

The program is a highly structured discussion group using psychodrama, music, magazines, videotapes, and movies. It is labelled 'personal awareness', or 'leadership training,' and is offered during study periods and before and after school. They give kids the truth about drinking and taking drugs, and then place the responsibility on them to make an informed choice. They make every attempt to communicate the dignity of the child to child, and make it known that he or she is lovable, valuable, and his or her health is essential and a primary consideration. This one program model has been extended to grammar schools and other high schools, with a number of men working on the streets in the evening hours in the community (Sr. Madeleine, 1984), (pp. 117-120).

Charles Crawford of The Gallo Winery believes we should focus on encouraging responsibility among young people rather than to force prevention. In the official driver's license handbook, some states include information relating to sanctions on drunk driving but not much about how much alcohol it takes to achieve a blood alcohol content that breaks the law, (BAC of 0.10 percent at present). He also suggests the inclusion of a Sunday comic each week regarding the need to understand temperance and self responsibility, geared to the 12-16-year olds.

Success of some programs does tend to have a catalytic effect. A number of approaches have proven helpful, such as media portrayal of alcohol consumption, beverage labeling, bartender liability and training, minimum age restrictions and other policy issues. Although community prevention efforts have usually focused on small-scale neighborhood problems, success in resolving issues of limited scope encourages a community to respond willingly to alcohol problems on a broader scope (Charles Crawford, 1984), (pp. 133-134).

Why Some Children Become Alcoholics

There is a tendency for some members of our present society to believe that alcoholism is hereditary, and they go no further for questioning any other variables as causes of alcoholism, directly or indirectly.

Since recent research reports that *most* children of alcoholics do not become alcoholic and *most* alcoholics do not have alcoholic parents (Fingarette, 1988), it is indicative of a need for further research on the social-psychological factors involved in the etiology of alcoholism. In some cases, there is a genetic basis for alcoholism (see Cloninger, 1987; Wilson & Crowe, 1991).

Ullman and Orenstein (1994) report that family rituals were either intact or disrupted; that mothers had either high or low esteem for their alcoholic husbands; that families were either high or low transmitters of alcoholism. They presented a less complex formulation, without expanding on gender, birth order, temperment of the child, location of drinking, and drinking style of the alcoholic parent. In so doing, they reported that strong motivation to drink among offspring of alcoholics is generated by families in which alcoholics have more power; thus leading to greater emulation and identification by children and adolescents, and through these processes offspring expect that alcohol will help them to be and to feel powerful. For social psychologists, this is an attractive formulation viewing the motivation to drink among children of alcoholics as an explicit social product dependent on learning processes within the family, and not necessarily the product of unspecified processes resulting from biological Inherltance (Ullman & Oicnstein, 1991).

Broadening the Base of Treatment for Alcohol Problems

The Committee of the Institute of Medicine - Division of Mental Health and Behavioral Medicine contracted with the National Institute on Alcohol Abuse and Alcoholism of the Department of Health and Human Services, who summarized their vision of treatment in a broadened sense (1990).

Each person presently has his/her own concept or belief about alcohol use as a beverage to be enjoyed, to be avoided, or to be removed from any marketplace. In many respects the treatment of alcohol problems is a rather recent phenomenon, but treatment in the United States can be traced back for almost 200 years.

There has been concern expressed by the U.S. Congress from time to time regarding treatment of people with alcoholism and by 1986 the report of

The House Committee on Energy and Commerce noted a need for treatment services to be emphasized in light of the nation's health care system. They authorized a study on the treatment of alcohol problems in Section 4022 of Public Law 99-570, the Alcohol, Drug Abuse and Mental Health Amendments of 1986 enacted in October of that year.

In Section 4022 the Secretary of Health and Human Services was required to arrange for specific research to be carried out through the direction of the National Institute on Alcohol Abuse and Alcoholism (NIAAA, 1990).

The overall focus included reviewing available research knowledge and experience in the United States and other countries regarding provision of treatment and rehabilitative services for alcoholism and alcohol abuse; assessment of comparative costs, quality, appropriateness and effectiveness of alcohol abuse treatment and rehabilitative services; the review of financing alternatives available to the public, including third-party insurers, and state and municipal governments; and recommendations for policies and programs of research, administration and reimbursement for the treatment of those individuals suffering from alcoholism and alcohol abuse.

The National Academy of Science was identified by Congress to carry out this study, while other related studies were in process related to various aspects of alcoholism and (treatment) approaches to the problems.

In 1987, the National Academy of Sciences accepted the responsibility for conducting the study. The National Academy of Science is a private, nonprofit corporation that was chartered by Abraham Lincoln in 1863 to provide advice to the government on matters of science and technology. Through the years, this group has developed interest in dealing with alcohol and drug problems.

The Committee addressed the vision or endpoint toward which treatment seems to be evolving and how it ought to evolve; providing answers to some fundamental questions about treatment; discussing certain aspects of the treatment process and what should require special attention; reviewing special populations in treatment; examining the financing of treatment and evaluating opportunities for leadership in the treatment area for the future.

From the discussions, it is obvious many treatment changes have occurred during the past 20 years and there are further questions to be addressed.

Treatment is sought and received in public installations as well as private facilities, and how much coercion to treatment is uncertain. There are differences between and among various treatment facilities, and it is difficult to know if there has been an expansion for treating new groups. Treatment outcome studies are lacking. It would seem that the alcohol treatment system has taken on a broad responsibility for major social problems of a diverse nature. The question is asked, what will be the long-term effects of the public image of the alcoholic or problem drinker - or the image of who belongs in treatment?

This paper attempted to identify some strong, basic similarities related to coercion in treatment that cut across public and private institutions and across the criminal justice and work-related referrals. It also noted that there are new populations in treatment, perhaps entering treatment earlier than previously and the diversity is invigorating the alcohol field and broadening its horizons. There are dilemmas and further questions that require the seeking of solutions to the problems in order to serve the field effectively (Institute of Medicine Committee, 1990).

Rural Drug and Alcohol Treatment

Based on data from the National Household Survey on Drug Abuse (1985) related to rural drug and alcohol abuse treatment, it was noted by (Edwards, 1992) that drug use in rural areas is substantial. Use of alcohol in rural areas does not differ from urban areas. It supports other studies reporting that marijuana and cocaine use are at lower levels in the real "true" rural areas.

Treatment differs between rural services and urban services since providers offer a wider array of interventions more focused on out-patient services.

Designing Treatment Programs

Use of tobacco and alcohol are popular in rural areas. There is a need to develop plans accordingly. There are more older residents and fewer minority residents in rural than in other areas, hence the treatment program needs expertise for treating an elderly group who seeks help. The rural treatment seekers use more alcohol than cocaine or marijuana.

According to The National Household Survey data, rural residents are reluctant to seek treatment, and rarely seek help for their addiction. Since their work pattern is less affected than urban abusers, an outreach for this group may be indicated to meet community drug and alcohol problems. Other identification methods may be used like the DWI programs, as one helpful way to plan for intervention.

The rural treatment program staff reported high level of heated arguments while people are drinking. Early identification could be developed through working with law enforcement officers to assist in intervention (Leukefeld et al, 1992, 95-117).

In reflecting data from the late 1980's and into the 1990's, the general trends in drug use of American youth continued to show some decrease each year, although small.

Use of marijuana in early 1990's may be lower than reported, but there has been only small changes in use from year to year.

A minimal difference is found in drug use of urban and rural youth, which is a change in the past fifteen years when drug abuse was an urban problem. From present knowledge it seems the use of drugs will not be too different for the two communities for the next few years. The small towns are somewhat more predictive in that the drug lifetime prevalence for almost every drug is slightly lower in the very small towns. The drugs will probably be available to teens living in small towns, just as they are for those teens living in the large cities. The geographic isolation and lower population density provide only a minimal protection to teens from drugs and alcohol exposure.

Since the taking of drugs seems to be a peer activity, the younger children may have less opportunity to mix with their peers without adults around. A large percentage live on farms where there are fewer children of their own age. By the time they are seniors in high school they are old enough to drive without supervision and they have more chance to socialize with other youth including the urban population. It is quite possible that some rural communities operate under the misconception that they are protected from social problems experienced in larger urban areas.

In both settings, rural and nonrural, males seem to have a slightly higher potential for drug involvement. The equivalent use of stimulants by females is an exception; when females use stimulants they use more than males. Females are frequently dieting and may use stimulants to suppress their appetites in some cases. When it comes to the consumption of alcohol, rural women are just as likely as urban women to use alcohol or other drugs. The implications for rural and urban youth may be different. Alcohol is the substance most heavily used among rural teens. The need for rural youth to spend more time on the road in travel may present an added problem. Distance, poor road conditions and higher speed all contribute to hazards for the rural teens.

Marijuana is the second most frequent used drug, which has a potential to distort judgment and the sense of time and motion, which interfere with competent driving. If and when it is used with alcohol the effect is worse for either substance used alone.

The major influences on drug involvement are family, school, and peer groups. In both rural and urban environments, a strong caring family with solid values helps to protect the youth from more serious drug involvement. The attitude of parents and their values concerning drug use do influence family members regardless of the size of the nearby community.

It can be concluded that predominant socializing forces leading to drug use are probably similar everywhere. Although there are some rural/urban differences, they are not the primary causes of drug use. The socializing forces, however, must be considered in prevention and treatment as the major social forces that relate to drug use interface differently with community systems and resources. For example, the links between families, peer groups, religion, schools, law enforcement, and recreation are different in the rural and urban communities. Therefore, efforts to deal with alcohol and drug problems must consider the unique needs and resources of a particular rural community. This is particularly true because of the lack in law enforcement and resources in the rural area. Rural towns may be different from each other and they may need programs tailored to each of them.

The school dropout rate of a particular town should be taken into consideration. If the dropout rate is high in a given community the increased

drug rate may be greater at the eighth grade level than in the 12th grade. Since the two populations of rural and nonrural have comparable rates of drug use, resources for prevention and treatment are important. Rural then should be given essentially equal priority for funding. Rural communities must not be ignored at the federal level when it comes to money for
prevention and treatment (Edwards, 1992).

The Use of Alcohol, Marijuana, and Hard Drugs by Rural Adolescents: A Review of Recent Resesearch

From 65 research reports or manuscripts on this topic of alcohol use, use of marijuana, and use of hard drugs by rural usage has shown that rural youth are closing the gap in reference to marijuana smoking.

With the exception of inhalants and stimulants, the use of hard drugs was lower among rural youth.

Donnermeyer (1992) made several recommendations for research to a better understanding of the similarity and differences of patterns between rural and nonrural populations. He suggests it is time to develop a new portrait of rural juvenile delinquents, since the use of illegal substances among rural youth has become a serious problem and he recommends,

1. Researchers need to go beyond correlational studies and apply criminology theory more systematically.

2. Community - neighborhood level factors need to be researched, for example, farm versus nonfarm residence, and cultural differences among Native American communities as important aspects for study.

3. A need for longitudinal designed studies relating to rural use of illicit substances.

4. A need to research the role of reference groups, (peers and adults) and

prevention programs as constraining or facilitating influences.

5. A greater need for study of relationship between ethnic and racial use among rural youth, and finally

6. The need for studying the relationship between substance use and particular sports, work, extra-curricular activities and non-school youth groups.

Although some activities might increase opportunities for use of drugs, the participation in other activities could constrain drug use (Donnermeyer, 1992), (Edwards (Ed.), (pp. 31-77).

Psychoactive Drug Use in the United States

There is an attempt to lump all types of psychoactive drugs together in one category and call them "drugs" or "dope". There is not a clear understanding as to why drugs are used, and Americans are perplexed as to management of the drug problem. Facts about the drug crisis are unclear. Perhaps going back to understanding what a psychoactive substance is would be helpful.

From Stephens (1992), we learn, a psychoactive substance is a chemical which has its most direct effect on the central nervous system. While these substances affect other parts of the body, for example narcotics slow the bowel motility and can be used to treat diarrhea, but their principal effect is on the brain. So, they affect mood and perception, and they have been used for many years by humankind just because they do alter emotions and perceptions.

Grouping these drugs by chemical structure and physiological effect, they are classified as:

(1) narcotics,

(2) generalized depressants,

(3) mood modifiers,

(4) hallucinogens, and

(5) stimulants.

Tolerance and Addiction

To comprehend effects of drugs, there is a need to understand related physiological processes of tolerance and addiction.

Tolerance is the mechanism whereby the body adjusts gradually to the level of the drug taken in. As tolerance is developed the user must ingest additional substance to induce that same feeling previously attained with a smaller quantity.

Addiction, then, is the process whereby the body becomes habituated to the drug physiologically. Addiction is recognized by the user's body reactions to the lack of the drug, and sometimes violently. In withdrawing from some drugs, for example narcotics is unpleasant but usually not life-threatening. On the other hand, withdrawal from barbiturates can result in death.

Most psychoactive drugs produce tolerance and this explains why many heavy and regular users continue to use an increasing amount of drugs (Stephens, 1992), (Mieczkowski (Ed.), (pp. 1-32). Psychoactive Drug Use in the United States Today: A Critical Review, Mieczkowski, T. (Ed) in *Drugs, Crime, and Social Policy*, Boston: Allyn & Bacon Publishers.

Drug User's World

Glassner and Loughlin (1987), describe the two models of drug use, epidemiological and political, based on assumptions related to the meaning of drug use for the users themselves. A correlate of increased use of marijuana and some of the other psychoactive drugs in the 1960's was development of a visible lifestyle, complimentary to drug use. Music, clothing, language and neighborhoods permitted researchers to locate and interact with drug users who described their behavior as positive who had support from a larger social group.

The adolescent drug use and adult concerns about the use have increased in the course of the century. Some dramatic changes have taken place in the lives of individuals between 12 and 20 during this period. Adolescence has been discovered as a developmental stage of life and determined as a social period with a distinctive style. It is in light of these changes that drug use, the distribution and effects can be understood.

Fears that parents held in 1920 about control of their young adult's behavior were enhanced by new occupational choices, urbanization and contact with drug use, along with religious and ethnic intermarriage, exposure to cultural challenges of education, and the development of youth-oriented music and clothing demonstrating a generation difference. All these changes were challenges not only to parents, but to teachers and employers who plan and work for cultural continuity. In the interactions with adolescents as part of this study, they often mentioned the fact that young adults live in a different time from their parents. The personal explorations in talking with adolescents themselves about their lives were quite different than most research studies (Glassner and Loughlin, 1987).

Treatment of Drug Addiction

According to (Roman, 1992), in the past there have been two major social policy approaches to the problem of drug abuse in our society. One centered on the supply side of drugs which emphasizes law enforcement, controlling production of drugs in other countries, intercepting drug supplies and applying punishment to those engaged in drug sales and distribution. The other approach is to reduce the demand for drugs.

Roman (1992) provides some historical background. He noted that the first sharp regard with drug abuse in America arose in the last quarter of the nineteenth century, at the close of the Civil War. During the earlier period physicians were helping opiate addicts through their withdrawal with no concern for the psychological aspects of the problem. In the earlier part of the twentieth century, there was some maintenance treatment for narcotic addicts while some treatment programs for opiate addiction were developed. There was a shift away from treatment in the early 1920's when the clinics for opiate addicts were closed. With this came a rising moral trend against the use of all drugs. Opiate addiction was then viewed as criminal behavior which led to attempting to prevent drug dependency and control availability of narcotics, and criminal penalties were enforced. The federal government established two hospitals for narcotic addicts -- one in Lexington, Kentucky, and another in Forth Worth, Texas. When federal prisoners were judged by the courts in need of treatment, they were referred to one of those installations instead of prisons. When space was available voluntary patients were admitted. Interventions in those hospitals is described by (Glasscote et al, 1972),(pp. 222-224).

The patient was withdrawn by use of subcutaneous injections of decreasing amounts of morphine over a ten-day period, generally. (In 1948 Methadone was substituted for morphine).

For those who wished to remain after withdrawal there was a period of several months vocational training and education provided with medical care in order to provide corrective living experience. These settings were approved for psychiatric residency training programs and individual and group psychotherapy was provided for some patients. Many patients left against medical advice and the majority relapsed to drug use after discharge.

In response to a heroin epidemic in urban areas with increased crime rate in the 1950's and 1960's, there was an increased interest in treatment related to the epidemic. Methadone maintenance programs were introduced and the concept of therapeutic communities became a reality. In the late 1970's there was evidence of drug dependency caused by nonopioids and these addicts also needed treatment. Out-patient drug-free treatment programs were developed.

Currently, drug treatment reflects four major modalities of treatment:

(1) detoxification,

(2) outpatient methadone maintenance,

(3) residential/therapeutic communities, and

(4) outpatient drug-free programs.

Other interventions include, use of narcotic antagonists, using drugs to block the physiological and psychological effects of drugs. Behavioral approaches as extinction of conditioned responses and Contingency contracting; Psychotherapy; Biofeedback, and Relaxation Therapy; Hypnosis; Acupuncture; Self-Help Groups and Aftercare; Self-help Groups as the "therapeutic community", and Aftercare by the service community (Roman, 1992).

Treatment Effectiveness

Based on the variety of treatments and complexities, and the lack of specificity of programs that have been studied, it is difficult to evaluate the effectiveness. And, as we practitioners know, not all clients respond to treatment in the same manner, which increases the need to utilize more than one treatment approach for some clients.

Some of those who deal with the drug dependent population believe that complete abstinence of mood-altering drugs is the only criterion for success. Realizing that drug abuse is a complex psychological, social, and physiological phenomenon, a number of researchers are looking into variables such as, interpersonal relationships, employment, general physical health, criminality, and general social functioning, as part of the outcome measurement for evaluating treatment programs (Roman, 1992).

REFERENCES

Boyd, Sr. Madeleine, (1984). What Schools Can Do: A Philadelphia Story. In Gerstein, S. (Ed.) *Toward the Prevention of Alcohol Problems.* (pp. 117-120). Washington, D.C.: National Academy Press.

Crawford, C. (1984). Comments on Alcohol, Youth, and Drunk Driving. In Gerstein, D. (Ed.) *Toward the Prevention of Alcohol Problems.* (pp. 133-134). Washington, D.C.: National Academy Press.

Denzin, N. (1987). *Treating Alcoholism.* California: Sage Publications, Inc.

Donnermeyer, J. (1992). Psychoactive Drug Use in the United States Today: A Critical Overview, (pp. 31-77). In Edwards, R. W. (Ed.) *Drug Use in Rural American Communities.* New York: The Haworth Press, Inc.

Edwards, R. W. (Ed.) (1992). *Drug Use in Rural American Communities.* New York: The Haworth Press, Inc.

Gerstein, D. (Ed.) (1984). *Toward the Prevention of Alcohol Problems.* Washington, D.C.: National Academy Press.

Glassner, B. and Loughlin, J. (1987). *Drugs in Adolescent Worlds* Burnouts to Straights. London: Macmillan Press.

Institute of Medicine (U.S.) Committee for the Study of Treatment and Rehabilitation Services for Alcoholism and Alcohol Abuse. (1990). *Broadening the Base of Treatment for Alcohol Problems.* Washington, D.C.: National Academy Press.

Leukefeld, C., Clayton, R., and Myers, J. (1992). Rural Drug and Alcohol Treatment. In Edwards, R. W. (Ed.) *Drug Use in Rural American Communities.* (pp. 95-117). New York: The Haworth Press, Inc.

Roman, S. (1992). The Treatment of Drug Addiction: An Overview. In Mieczkowski, T. (Ed.) *Drugs, Crime, and Social Policy.* (pp. 222-250). Boston: Allyn and Bacon Publishers.

Schuchard, K. (1984). Alcohol, Youth, Drunk Driving. In Gerstein, D. (Ed.) *Toward the Prevention of Alcohol Problems.* (pp. 110-117). Washington, D.C.: National Academy Press.

Stephens, R. C. (1992). Psychoactive Drug Use in the United States Today: A Critical Overview. In Mieczkowski, T. (Ed.) *Drugs, Crime, and Social Policy.* (pp. 1-32). Boston: Allyn and Bacon Publishers.

Ullman, A. and Orenstein, A. (1994). Why Some Children Become Alcoholics: Emulation Of The Drinker. *Adolescence.* 29 (113), 1-10.

CHAPTER X

The Depressions

Basic terminology, classifications and definitions are described in the *Diagnostic and Statistical Manual of Mental Disorders.* DSM-III-R (3rd. ed. Revised 1987).

MOOD DISORDERS

The essential feature of the following group of disorders is a disturbance of mood, accompanied by a full or partial Manic or Depressive Syndrome (not due to any other physical or mental disorder). Mood refers to a prolonged emotion that colors the whole psychic life; it generally involves either depression or elation. (Formerly referred to as Affective Disorders).

The subclassification of Mood Disorders is as follows:

1.   Bipolar Disorders

2.   Depressive Disorders

(1) Bipolar Disorders - the essential feature is the presence of one

---

American Psychiatric Association (1987). *Diagnostic and Statistical Manual of Mental Disorders.* DSM-III-R (3rd. ed. Revised 1987). Reprinted by Permission of the American Psychiatric Association, Washington, D.C.

or more Manic or Hypomanic Episodes (usually with a history of Major Depressive episodes).

(2) Depressive Disorders - the essential feature is one or more periods of depression without a history of either Manic or Hypomanic Episodes.

    1 (a)   There are two Bipolar Disorders - in which there is one or more Manic Episodes (usually with one or more Major Depressive Episodes; and

    1 (b) Cyclothymia, in which there are numerous Hypomanic Episodes and numerous periods with depressive symptoms.

There are two Depressive Disorders:

2 (a) Major Depression, in which there is one or more Major Depressive Episodes; and

2 (b) Dysthymia, in which there is a history of a depressed mood more days than not for at least two years and in which, during the first two years of the disturbance, the condition did not meet the criteria of a Major Depressive Episode. (In many cases of Dysthymia, there are superimposed Major Depressions).

Note: If the criteria for a Major Depression or Manic Episode are currently met, the episode is subclassified as, mild, moderate, or severe without psychotic features, or with psychotic features.

A current Major Depressive Episode can be specified as:

Melancholic type - a form of a Major Depressive Episode believed to be partially due to somatic therapy; or

Chronic - the current episode lasted two consecutive years without a period of two months or longer in which there have been no depressive symptoms.

For *Bipolar Disorder, (Not otherwise specified, NOS)*

Recurrent Depression and Depressive Disorder (NOS), a further specification is:

Seasonal pattern - a regular cyclic relationship between onset of the mood episodes and a particular 60-day period of the year.

Manic Episode

The essential feature of a Manic Episode is a distinct period during which the predominant mood is elevated, expansive, *or* irritable, and there are associated symptoms of the Manic Syndrome. The disturbance is severe enough to cause marked impairment in one's occupational functioning or in their usual social activities or relationships with others, or possibly requiring hospitalization to prevent harm to self or to others.

Associated symptoms include inflated self-esteem or grandiosity (may be delusional), decreased need for sleep, pressured speech, flight of ideas, distractibility, increased involvement in goal-directed activity, psychomotor agitation, and excessive involvement in pleasurable activities which have a great potential for painful consequences, sometimes not recognized by the person.

The diagnosis is made only if it cannot be established that an organic factor, either initiated and/or maintained the disturbance. Neither is this diagnosis made if the disturbance is superimposed on Schizophrenia, Schizophreniform Disorder, Delusional Disorder, or Psychotic Disorder NOS, or if the criteria for Schizoaffective Disorder are met.

Although the elevated mood is considered the prototype symptom, the predominant mood disturbance may be irritability, which could be most apparent when the person is thwarted.

Other symptoms previously listed are self-explanatory, but it is well to note the problem of distractibility usually present, evidenced by rapid changes in speech or activity, resulting from their responding to irrelevant external stimuli, such as background noise, or signs or pictures on the wall.

In regards to the increase in goal-directed activity it may involve excessive planning of, and participation in, multiple activities (e.g. sexual, occupational, political, or religious).

Frequently, there is lack of judgment in buying sprees, reckless driving, unwise business investments, and sexual behavior unusual for the person. Their dress may reflect excessive style and color, to name some of the obvious symptoms of the Manic Episode (APA, 987, p.214).

Hypomanic Episode

The essential feature of a Hypomanic Episode is a distinct period in which the predominant mood is elevated, expansive, *or* irritable with associated features of the Manic Syndrome. Usually, by definition, the disturbance is not severe enough to cause marked impairment in the social or occupational functioning or to require hospitalization, (as required in the diagnosis of a Major Episode).

Associated features of Hypomanic Episodes are similar to a Manic Episode except that delusions are never present and other symptoms tend to be less severe than in Manic Episodes (APA, 1987, p.218).

BIPOLAR DISORDERS

Mixed

Manic

Depressed

Cyclothymia - Major feature is a chronic mood disturbance, of at least two years' duration (one year for children and adolescents), involving numerous Hypomanic Episodes and numerous periods of depressed mood or loss of interest or pleasure, duration and severity to meet criteria for a Major Depressive or a Manic Episode.

Bipolar Disorder (NOS)

Disorders with manic or hypomanic features that do not meet criteria for any specific Bipolar Disorder (APA, 1987, pp. 213 - 225).

Major Depressive Episode

The essential feature of a Major Depressive Episode is either a depressed mood (possibly, an irritable mood in children and adolescents); or loss of interest or pleasure in almost all activities, and associated symptoms, for at least two weeks. The symptoms represent a definite change from previous functioning, and are persistent, in that they occur for most of the day, nearly every day during the two-week period.

Associated symptoms include disturbance of appetite, change in weight, sleep disturbance, psychomotor agitation or retardation, decreased energy, feelings of worthlessness or excessive or inappropriate guilt, difficulty in thinking or concentrating, recurrent thoughts of death, or suicidal ideation or attempts.

The diagnosis is made only if it cannot be established that an organic factor initiated *or* maintained the disturbance, and the disturbance is not a normal reaction to the loss of a loved one.

In addition, the diagnosis is not made if the disturbance is superimposed on Schizophrenia, Schizophreniform Disorder, Delusional Disorder, or Psychotic Disorder NOS, or if the criteria for Schizoaffective Disorder are met.

A person with a depressed mood usually describes feeling depressed, sad, discouraged, hopeless, "down in the dumps", and the person may look sad and depressed. The family will notice their withdrawal from friends and family and lack of interest in avocations once enjoyed.

In addition to a common loss of appetite followed by weight loss, there is commonly disturbance in the sleep pattern. Initially, the person may have difficulty falling asleep, or have early morning awakening with difficulty in falling back to sleep. Hypersomnia may involve sleeping for longer periods of time than usual.

Frequently, the sleep disturbance is the main symptom that brings the person into treatment.

The sense of worthlessness varies from feelings of inadequacy to completely unrealistic negative evaluation of one's worth. Guilt may be expressed to past failings or as an exaggerated responsibility for a tragic event. The sense of worthlessness or guilt may be of delusional proportions.

Thoughts of death are common. There is often the belief that the person or others would be better off dead. There may be suicidal thoughts, with or without a plan, or suicide attempts (APA, 1987, pp.218-219).

DEPRESSIVE DISORDERS

Major Depression, single episode

Major Depression, Recurrent

Dysthymia (or Depressive Neurosis)

Essential feature is a chronic disturbance of mood involving depressed mood (possibly an irritable mood in children and adolescents) most of the day for more days than not, for at least two years (one year for children or adolescents).

Some of the following symptoms are associated during these periods of depressed mood, poor appetite, insomnia or hypersomnia, low energy or fatigue, low self-esteem, poor concentration or difficulty making decisions, and feelings of hopelessness.

Depressive Disorder (NOS) - disorders with depressive features that do not meet the criteria for any specific Mood Disorder or Adjustment Disorder with Depressed Mood.

Examples:

(1) a Major Depressive Episode superimposed on residual Schizophrenia;

(2) a recurrent, mild, depressive disturbance that does not meet the criteria for Dysthymia;

(3) non-stress-related depressive episodes that do not meet the criteria for a Major Depressive Episode (APA, 1987, pp.213-233).

Depression in Children and Adolescents

The literature seems to pose more questions than answers at present, but as more research of children and adolescents is completed relating to depression, there will be a better understanding of affective disorders in children.

According to (Schacter and Romano, 1993), the evaluation of the child for depression, the criteria across ages should include,

affective (dysphoria, weepiness, mood change and anhedonia;

cognitive (low self esteem, hopelessness, and helplessness;

vegetative (sleep and appetite disturbances); and

motivational (anergia, decreased social interactions, and avoidance) symptoms with additional specific criteria for young children. (Currently depression in children can be diagnosed according to the criteria

J.E. Schacter and B.A. Romano (1993). Developmental Issues in Childhood and Adolescent Depression. In Koplewicz, H.S. and Klass, E. (Eds.) *Depression in Children and Adolescents*. Chur, Switzerland: Gordon and Breach Publishing Group. Reprinted by Permission of Gordan & Breach Publishing Group.

used in diagnosing adult depression).

Infancy and Preschool years

As early as infancy depressive-like behaviors can be observed. In Spitz's term 'anaclitic depression', was in reference to weepiness, the withdrawal, apathy, weight loss, sleep disturbance, developmental decrements in six to twelve-month old institutionalized infants (Spitz, 1946).

Bowlby (1960) described his observation sequence of protest - despair - detachment in toddlers, ages six months to four years, separated from maternal caretakers. There is some question if these are true depression examples, or rather a parallel to adult grief reactions. At any rate, it cannot be denied these infants are experiencing negative affective changes which can become disabling.

For the preschooler, researchers have used grief reactions as a model for studying depression. It has been found that their grief reactions are milder and of shorter duration than older children.

School-Aged Years

Most of the research on child depression has been focused on school-aged children. As already stated, consensus is that depression is the period that parallels depression in the adult population.

Adolescence

As children mature cognitively, socially, and physiologically into adolescence, depressive symptoms are more typical of what is observed in adults. An important aspect to consider is differentiation between 'normal' adolescent turmoil and psychopathology. Emphasis is placed on duration of symptoms, severity, and the combination of symptoms in attempting to diagnose depression in this age group.

Many questions are raised from the above review, since we don't fully understand how the syndrome of depression is affected by the developmental progression (Ed.) Koplewicz, H.S. & Klass, E, 1993)(pp.1-11).

Present State of Biology in Depression

It was concluded by Gjerris et al (1991) that several lines of evidence do support existence of a genetic factor related to depression; dysfunctions in the biogenic amine systems and hormones do seem likely; however, there are no convincing results finally verifying these hypotheses as yet. The evidence is strong that present lack of success probably is due to our simplistic mode of thinking and inadequate technology at this time. It is recommended that the biology of depression, the complexity of the neurotransmitter system and interactions between systems be studied intensively on a longitudinal basis in future research. Techniques such as brain imaging, methods to measure receptor function, and molecular biology, along with a less simplistic way of considering character of dysfunctions may assist us with the answers (Gjerris et al, 1991, p.59).

Depression Prevention Research

As we approach the end of the twentieth century, it is obvious that the mental health field has successfully demonstrated that a number of human maladies can be considered as psychological or psychiatric disorders. The classification of psychological disorders has been collaborative across the globe.

Treatment methods have progressed according to documented examples

A. Gjerris et al (1991). The Present State of Biology in Depression. In Per Krag-Sorenson (Eds.). Gjerris, A. and Bolwig, T.G. *Depression*, 46-63. Reprinted by Permission, Munksgaard International Publishers Ltd. Copenhagen, Denmark.

of effectiveness; there has also been progress in identification and treatment of psychological problems, with need for additional progress.

The endeavor in prevention of psychological problems is still in its infancy. There are some pioneering practitioners attempting preventive interventions, and a small number of researchers who are studying preventive intervention experimentally, which may well set the pace for outstanding advances in the twenty-first century.

Prevention efforts are generally divided into three levels:

Primary prevention - to reduce incidence of the disorder or number of new cases;

Secondary prevention - involves early identification and treatment of cases, attempting to reduce prevalence; and

Tertiary prevention - focuses on reducing disability as a result of full-blown cases with the disorder, frequently called rehabilitation. So, it would seem that primary prevention should be the only one referred to as prevention, and secondary and tertiary should be referred to as treatment and rehabilitation.

Important elements in depression prevention research projects, according to (Munoz, 1987), should include defining the target for intervention, specifying theorized mechanisms underlying the chosen approach, identifying details of intervention method to be evaluated, and measuring short- and long-term effects of intervention on theorized mechanisms and the ultimate target (Munoz, 1987).

R.F. Munoz (1987). Depression Prevention Research: Conceptual and Practical Consideration. In Munoz, R.F. (Ed) *Depression Prevention Research Directions* (3-31). Bristol, PA: Hemisphere Publishing Corp. Reprinted by Permission of Hemisphere Publishing Corporation.

How to Deal With Depression — Treatment and Coping

According to (DePaulo and Ablow, 1989), once a diagnosis of an affective disease or disorder is made today, the psychiatrist proposes a treatment plan, and then tailors the treatment to the patient, taking the individual history and needs into consideration.

The Role of Psychotherapy

There are different kinds of psychotherapy, although all forms involve a confiding relationship between a professional therapist and a patient, that allows the patient's experiences and life predicaments to be shared.

Supportive Psychotherapy

The most widely applicable form of psychotherapy for affective disorders is supportive psychotherapy. This therapy seeks to convey realities about depression to patients whose abilities to understand their illnesses are impaired. It helps to bolster self-confidence and self-esteem; it helps to promote the patient's best psychological and social functioning; it helps to make the patient aware of what can and cannot be done -- limitations of the individual and limitations of treatment; it helps to prevent unnecessary dependency on professional support and unnecessary hospitalization; and it helps to promote the best use of available support from family and friends.

Cognitive Therapy

The goal of cognitive therapy is designed to correct negative thinking

J. DePaulo & K.P. Ablow (1989). *How to Cope with Depression.* pp. 133; 146-157. New York: McGraw-Hill Publishing Co., (c) (1989). Reprinted by Permission of McGraw-Hill, Inc.

158

habits, which lessen depressed feelings. It usually involves the therapist confronting the patient with the person's distortions in his/her image or view of the world.

Interpersonal Therapy

The therapist using interpersonal therapy is concerned with the here and now. The goal is to reestablish relationships between the depressed person and others by counseling the patient, and at times friends or family. As social functioning improves, the symptoms of depression, hopefully, will fade.

Behavioral Therapy

Behavioral Therapists attempt to extinguish the patient's negative behaviors and they try to maximize the reinforcement of positive behaviors.

Psychoanalytic Therapy

This type therapy, originally developed by Sigmund Freud, seeks to get at the unconscious conflicts which are believed to contribute to psychiatric symptoms. This type therapy can last for years.

Recommended Caution

Caution is emphasized in that psychotherapy has not shown a great success used alone for severe depression. When psychotherapy is part of the treatment regime, it is expected that patients will attend regularly scheduled therapy sessions.

Drug Therapy

Since the late 1950's, tricyclic antidepressants have been used for depressed patients of moderate to severe intensity, along with psychotherapy.

Monoamine Oxidase, listed as an inhibitor - one kind of noncyclic medication sometimes used as an antidepressant. Patients who take Monoamine Oxidase Inhibitors or (MAOIs) may experience some side effects as those taking tricyclic antidepressants.

A very important note accompanies these drugs, that patients have a restricted diet to avoid the risk of hypertensive crisis - a sudden increase in blood pressure. This would be due to an accumulation of an amino acid called *tyramine*, that occurs naturally in some foods, (such as cheeses and red wines, plus other foods). Usually there is no problem because it would be broken down by Monoamine Oxidase. With the enzyme inhibited, the amino acid can accumulate to dangerous levels.

Patients are also alerted to avoid certain drugs when taking MAOIs, so their physicians must instruct them carefully as individuals, if they are prescribed one of the MAOIs.

Lithium, a naturally occurring salt, was discovered by Dr. John Cade in 1949. Dr. Cade, an Australian psychiatrist, learned that it relieved symptoms of Mania. It has been used for mania and depression and it has become a major long-term therapy to ward off recurrences of either mood disorder, which tends to stabilize the moods of affectively ill patients.

Benzodiazapines, including Valium and Librium have long been used for treating anxiety.

Stimulants sometimes work when other medications do not work but frequently carry a risk of dependence along with some side effects.

Other Therapies

Electroconvulsive therapy (ECT) at times is used in treatment for severe depression. Usually it is used when drug therapy has failed, or when the patient is a high suicidal risk or starvation, or when the depressed person is troubled by delusions or hallucinations.

Phototherapy and Sleep Therapies

Researchers at the National Institute of Mental Health treated people suffering from seasonal depression with exposure to bright light for several hours each day. The treatment helped within the first week, with a rapid relapse after stopping the treatment.

Hopefully, current and future research will bring us new and even more innovating treatments for depressed patients (DePaul & Ablow, 1989).

Physical Health Impairment and Depression Among Older Adults

Badger (1993) addressed the differences among chronically ill older adults for physical health impairment, mastery, social support, which included social resources, economic resources, and depression. In addition, the study asked what factors are significant predictors of depression among chronically ill older adults. The convenience sample included 25 males and 55 females, white older adults living independently, and ages ranged from 60-75 years. Fifty-six per cent of the participants were married; Thirty-one per cent were widowed, and the rest were divorced or never married. Participants were fairly well educated, with forty-nine percent attending or completing high school; forty percent had post-high school education while eleven percent of the participants had less than eight years of formal education. All participants were retired. For

---

T.A. Badger (1993). Physical Health Impairment and Depression Among Older Adults. *Image* 25 (4), 325-331. Reprinted by Permission of Sigma Theta Tau, International Honor Society of Nursing Inc., Image Publication Office, Indianapolis, IN.

their occupations, thirty-five percent were clerical or in sales, while fifteen percent were managers or proprietors; ten percent were professionals, and nine percent were unskilled laborers.

The median income range was $15,000 to $19,999 per year. The most commonly cited sources of income were Social Security and Retirement Pensions. All reported one or more chronic illness such as arthritis, diabetes mellitus or hypertension, and they were being treated with medication for their conditions.

Their depression was measured using the Center for Epidemiological Studies - Depression Scale (CESD; Radloff, 1977). It is a 20-item self-report questionnaire that assesses frequency and severity of the depressed mood, their feelings of guilt and worthlessness, hopelessness, and helplessness, disturbances of sleep and appetite, and loss of energy.

Ultimately, the group of individuals were divided into two groups. Group (1) = 41 had mild physical health impairment and Group (2) = 38 had moderate to severe physical health impairment. There were no differences found between the groups for types of illnesses; however, there were significant differences for the subjective assessment of how much the illness impeded their daily functioning. This has implication for nursing practice since nurses can educate patients about specific techniques to help improve their ability to do things deemed important by the patient.

Social resources, economic resources and mastery were significant predictors of depression among these participants. The majority of participants in both groups reported that their income was not adequate for the future but it was sufficient to meet current daily needs.

Sixteen percent in Group (2) reported they had a drinking problem which was higher than reported earlier (fourteen percent for males and 1.5 percent for

162

females) reported by (Miller, 1991). This indicates a need for assessing for a drinking problem routinely.

Group (1) had 26 percent depressed, that indicated there were additional stressors present, not necessarily measured by this study.

Badger suggests that future research should include stressful life events and other factors that may be specific to older adults. The length of retirement and time they were suffering with the illness, or any change in the illness course could affect the outcome. The nursing research focused on how to enhance and modify personal and environmental resources.   This is part of nursing intervention to prevent depression in older adults or alleviate the depression of those individuals suffering from one or more chronic illnesses (Badger, 1993).

REFERENCES

American Psychiatric Association. (1987). *Diagnostic and Statistical Manual of Mental Disorders.* DSM-III-R (3rd. Ed). Washington, D.C.: American Psychiatric Association.

Badger, T.A. (1993). Physical Health Impairment and Depression Among Older Adults. *Image* 25 (4), 325-331.

DePaulo, J. and Ablow, K.P. (1989). How *to Cope With Depression.* New York: McGraw-Hill Publishing Company.

Gjerris et al, A. (1991) The Present State of Biology in Depression. In Per Kragh-Sorenson (Eds) Gjerris, A. and Bolwig, T.G. *Depression,* 46-63.

Muñoz, R.F. (1987). Depression Prevention Research: Conceptualand Practical Consideration. In Muñoz, R.F. (Ed). *Depression Prevention Research Directions.* Hemisphere Publishers Corp. 3-31.

Schacter, J.E. and Romano, B.A. (1993). Developmental Issues in Childhood and Adolescent Depression. In Koplewicz, H.S. and Klass, E. (Eds) *Depression in Children and Adolescents.* Chur, Switzerland: Gordan & Breach Publishing Group 1-15.

SUGGESTED READINGS

Bowlby, J. (1960). Separation anxiety. *International Journal of Psychoanalysis.* 41, 89-113.

Spitz, R. (1946) Anaclitic depression. *Psychoanalytic Study of the Child,* 2, 113-117.

CHAPTER XI

The Abusive Family

By

Marietta P. Stanton, Ph.D., R.N.
and
Ann Seidl, Ph.D., R.N.

INTRODUCTION

The family is the basic unit of society and the primary arena for personal socialization. Therefore, it has a profound effect on individual development. Society, in general, has certain expectations regarding individual behavior. The family and its individual members have respective needs and demands that must be met within the context of these societal expectations. The family must be able to balance individual members' demands and needs in alignment with society's demands in a healthy, constructive manner. If the family cannot manage to educate members appropriately to function in society, then varying degrees of individual and family dysfunction can emerge.

Dysfunctional behavior in any one family member can disrupt the lives and damage the health and welfare of other individuals within that family. This may interfere with the family's ability as a unit to interact in a healthy manner with society. A family member's dysfunction can also be the culmination of the entire family's stress. The literature suggests that "acting out" behaviors by one member may be a pressure release for the whole family. Dysfunction can also result when a specific member doesn't meet society's expectations for behavior in various arenas such as in school or on the job. This in turn has an impact on the quality of family life.

Family interactions and roles, communication techniques involving power, decision-making, and problem solving, as well as the expression of feelings and individuality, are crucial to family life, and therefore, individual behavior and development. Family life may seem "normal" or appear to adequately support its members to the outside observer. However, there may be varying degrees or different types of family dysfunction that compromise the health and welfare of members. Family dysfunction may also be covert in cases of emotional abuse or neglect and can occur on an escalating or diminishing continuum. On the other hand, this dysfunction can be manifested by overt signs of family distress as is seen in physical or domestic violence.

The composition of the basic family unit has changed in recent years. There are many single parent households. However, the family's role in preparing individuals to function successfully in society and nurturing self-esteem has not changed. The family that fosters constructive development of self help facilitates socially acceptable coping behavior in its members. The family that fosters the development of destructive behaviors usually manifests some level of dysfunction. The more extreme, prolonged forms of family dysfunction may result in an abusive and even violent family. Because violence is dangerous and may be life-threatening, the short term consequences and long term effects on individual behavior and welfare seem most obvious. However, emotional abuse in and of itself can be as destructive to one's self-concept and cripple an individual's ability to appropriately function in society throughout a lifetime.

There are many learned responses to the abuse which takes place within the family. Examining these learned responses and how they affect the health, welfare, behavior and socialization of family members will be the focus of the presentation. Any discussion, must first focus on family violence, the most profound result of dysfunction and the most obvious type of an abusive situation.

Family violence is a fact of life in every community whether it be rural or urban, affluent or poor. Approximately 34 percent of the population according to Family Violence Prevention Fund Survey have witnessed an incident of domestic violence (NYSNA, 1993). This hidden epidemic has recently come to the forefront of interventive efforts by health care professionals and institutions. Estimates about the incidence and prevalence of all types of family violence may be misleading because many incidents may not be reported. However, about half of the homicide victims in this country are killed by people they know (Sabatino, 1992) and many involve physical conflict between immediate or extended family members. To add to this, it is estimated that over one million children are abused annually (Stanton, 1990). Therefore, public opinion and statistics substantiate the magnitude of the problem. The increased prevalence of suicide in young adults has also been linked to a victim's history and exposure to family violence (Charles, 1991). There are many other examples of the negative effects of family or domestic violence on the physical and emotional health and welfare of family members.

Because family violence is an "ugly" aspect of our society, too often society is unresponsive. Even so, nine out of ten people in this country believe it is a primary public health problem (NYSNA, 1993). Proactive efforts to curtail family or domestic violence have included educating health professionals about its causes and consequences as well as community-based education for schoolteachers, police, lawyers, and judges regarding effective intervention. In many states, laws have been enacted which mandate the reporting of child abuse by selected professionals as well as education for these professionals to make them more effective at intervening in these situations. It is imperative that nurses as the largest group of health care professionals understand the profound effect this family violence has on the welfare, development, and maturation of individual family members. Domestic violence usually includes spousal battering. However, this violence can involve physical abuse of children and elders in the home as well. More and more frequently, violence is occurring between older and younger siblings. Many varied factors result in family violence but it is also associated with a variety of other contributing factors such as alcohol and drug abuse, poverty, and unemployment.

In addition to overt manifestations of physical abuse as seen in different types of family violence, there is a whole gamut of emotionally abusive behaviors that can occur within a dysfunctional family. Some of these emotionally abusive behaviors are obvious such as verbal threats or berating comments aimed at an individual family member. Other types of abuse might be less obvious such as a parent's indifference to the child's physical and emotional needs as is seen in cases of maltreatment and neglect. The negative effects of these types of abuse may not be noticed until extensive damage is done to the individual's self-concept or physical health.

Rape, incest, and sexual abuse can occur between family members. This has a tremendous impact on the victim. It can occur over a prolonged period and have devastating consequences to other family members as well as the victim. Even if the sexual abuse occurs outside the home at the hand of strangers, it can cause disruption of family life and function. These and other types of overt abuse will be discussed later.

In summary, families exhibit a wide variety of abusive behaviors, and families that do usually share some degree of dysfunction in basic familial relations. In the following presentation, the abusive family and its effect on learning and behavior will be examined.

Overview of the Model for Examining the Abusive Family

A model for the abusive family has been proposed by Stanton (1993). This model is based on the assumptions that individuals within a family each have unique individual needs, characteristics, and demands. The individual characteristics and needs in this model are classified as biological, cognitive-affective, behavioral, and sociological. The combination of individual member characteristics produces a distinct, unique person and the interaction of family members produces a unique family unit. In the abusive family, dysfunctional relationships interfere with the satisfaction of individual needs and demands. To cope, family members may employ a variety of unhealthy behaviors. Over time and without intervention, these unhealthy behaviors can become repetitive, negative patterns of response to societal norms. Therefore, reviewing characteristics of individual family members may pinpoint sources of dysfunction that affect the entire family.

Another aspect of individual behavior is motivation. Needs and demands vary according to an individual's motivational systems. Therefore, not only do individual characteristics affect family interaction but also the motivational system for each person. Once this is accomplished, one must look at the family as a total unit.

The family as a total unit exhibits distinct patterns of interaction as a whole with their environment. These interactive patterns may be healthy or dysfunctional or on some point along a continuum of health and dysfunction. This dysfunction represents an imbalance between family needs and demands, and the expectations of society. Dysfunctional interactive patterns between family members may result in different forms of abuse or violence. A mismatch between family needs, demands, and societal expectations can actually produce or intensify this internal dysfunction. Interactive patterns associated with a particular family unit can be altered and modulated by a multitude of factors and resources outside the family unit. Patterns can vary across time or remain relatively stable. The characteristics of individuals within the family combine to produce a unique family. The resulting family "portrait" in this model is described by selected parameters for family assessment suggested by Friedman (1981). The parameters drawn from Friedman's assessment criteria are family structure; family function; general characteristics or family traits; as well as the family's external environment. These parameters will assist in examining the family as a whole, different from the sum of individual characteristics of its members.

When a family is exposed to various life stresses or crises, this distinct family system can, as previously mentioned, interact with the environment as well as each other using healthy or unhealthy response patterns. Unhealthy response patterns may have negative short and long-term behavioral, physical, and emotional outcomes for all family members. These stresses and events are depicted in one of the middle circles of the model. The ability of the family to cope with these stressors, either internal or external, produces different kinds of outcomes. Short term outcomes in the abusive and dysfunctional family may include physical, cognitive, emotional, and behavioral sequelae. The long term consequences of exposure to violence or abuse is dependent on many variables and may be modified by positive intervening forces or buffering mechanisms that occur concurrently with the violence or abuse. The long-term behavioral, physical, and emotional outcomes of living within an abusive family then contribute to the intergenerational transmission of negative values and norms for behavior, coping and interaction with society. These values and norms fostered within the abusive family can be affected by the duration and frequency of abuse or violence, age of occurrence, short-term consequences, and buffering mechanisms. Families which are abusive and/or violent are obviously dysfunctional and have inadequate and inappropriate coping mechanisms to deal with life events and stressors. Because the family is the primary educator of children, a child may learn socially unacceptable behaviors and unhealthy coping styles in the dysfunctional and abusive family.

The individual components of the model will now be explored in more detail (See Figure I). This model will allow a more indepth examination of the potential characteristics of individuals within an abusive family as a whole, the learned responses to abuse or violence, the internal and external stressors, buffers, and the potential short and long-term outcomes of life in the abusive family.

Individual Characteristics

The family is a system and this system includes separate individuals who have unique behavioral, cognitive-affective, biological, and sociological characteristics which in-turn affect their interactions within the family and with society (Milner & Chilamkurti, 1991). These four sets of factors comprise the inner "core" of this present model (see Figure I). Milner and Chilamkurti's classification (1991) of predisposing factors for physical abuse perpetrators has been used as a framework for describing individual family member characteristics in this present model describing the abusive family and its members. The scope of this classification system has been expanded in this present discussion so that perpetrators, victims of all ages, and all types of family dysfunction, abuse, and violence are addressed. This approach will help identify individual characteristics which promote the dysfunction so often seen between the members of an abusive family. It will also illustrate how dysfunction affects the development of individual characteristics and how this in turn affects family member's subsequent interaction with society.

Biological Factors

Biological characteristics can produce certain types of physiological responses to stimuli. For instance, in one study, physical abusers of children were found to have different skin surface reactions to child related stimuli than non abusers (Friedrich, Tyler, & Clark, 1985).

Neurological and neuropsychological factors, a set of biological characteristics, can also affect the way input from the environment is processed by an individual. Therefore, neurological factors mediate the responses to that input. Neuropathology might cause the data to be interpreted in a negative way. This misinterpretation of input might stimulate individual dysfunction and provide negative consequences for other family members. Biological factors have been used to explain why perpetrators use violent, coercive behaviors when their personal childhood history does not include victimization.

Physical health can affect perception and responses to stimuli. In fact, physical illnesses, and somatic illnesses are seen with increased frequency in child abuse perpetrators (Lahey, Conger, Atkenson, & Trieber, 1984). Having a disabling illness or being physically challenged may place children at higher risk for abuse (Miller, Fine, & Adams-Taylor, 1989). Gender, appearance, and other biological characteristics have been linked to victim and perpetrator profiles (Miller, et al, 1989). Therefore, the biological characteristics of an individual family member, even from these few examples, can disrupt family life and can enhance a family member's potential for violence or abuse either as a victim or a victimizer.

Cognitive-Affective Factors

Characteristics of the individual associated with cognitive and affective (attitude) function are also factors in the evolution of family abuse and/or violence. One of these, self-esteem, has an effect on how individuals deal and cope with stress. Individuals with low-self esteem handle stress in inappropriate as well as socially unacceptable ways. At times, individuals use violence as a method for handling stress (Widom, 1989). Abusive parents tend to suffer from low self-esteem (Steele, 1987). A low self-esteem as a result of abuse, maltreatment, or neglect has been linked with suicide, depression (Charles, 1991), juvenile delinquency (Widom, 1992), substance abuse (Charles, 1991), poor school and job performance (Stanton, 1990), and a host of other long-term dysfunctional behaviors. Alternatively, a healthy self-esteem seems to even reduce one's risk for accidental injury and violent crime (Stanton, 1990). Individuals with low self-esteem also seem unable to handle interpersonal conflict in a socially acceptable manner. This affects interaction with the family and with society. This is evidenced by the fact that many assault and homicide perpetrators tend to suffer from a diminished self-concept and low self-esteem (Widom, 1989). Self-esteem is primarily developed, learned and nurtured within the family environment. If the family is abusive and the parents themselves suffer from the behavioral sequelae of low self-esteem, children developing in that environment may not develop a healthy self-concept. These children additionally learn their parent's unhealthy patterns of response when their self-esteem is threatened. Therefore, self-esteem decidedly evolves within the family unit and the abusive family erodes self-esteem. The family as a whole, in turn, is affected by the self-esteem of all its members.

Another individual cognitive affective factor affected by and affecting the family environment is the set of responses associated with locus of control. Actual and potential physical child abusers appear to have an external locus of control that includes control by powerful others (Stringer & LaGreca, 1985). Parents who abuse children tend to project responsibility for their violent behavior on external factors, including the child (Milner & Chilamkurti, 1991). This external locus of control is also a factor in spousal and elder abuse. The externality seen in abusive or violent individuals has been related to the victimizer's own history of parental rejection, lack of warmth, and abuse. Therefore, an external locus of control as a set of response patterns is learned and regenerated within the abusive family environment. The externality seen in family violence also encourages the transmission of intergenerational violence as well as an ongoing cycle of family dysfunction.

Another individual cognitive-affective factor, applicable to all types of abuse, especially spousal, is learned helplessness (Joyce, 1993). With learned helplessness, both the perpetrator and victim seem governed by externality. The victim feels unable to deal with the abuse and the victimizer projects blame on the victim.

Other types of individual cognitive affective factors which affect family violence are the perceptions, evaluations and expectations related to behavior that individual family members have for each other. For instance, abusive parents tend to have significant misconceptions concerning the appropriateness of their child's behavior and tend to see more of that child's behavior as negative (Pollock & Steele, 1972). Also, abusive parents usually have very unrealistic expectations of their child's abilities and seem to lack empathy for the child's developmental needs (Stanton, 1990). Abusive parents may fear spoiling the child and have a strong belief in the value of severe physical punishment (Hawkins, 1986). This and other unhealthy patterns of child rearing are learned within the abusive family and may be perpetuated from one generation to the next if there are no outside influences or interventions to buffer the unhealthy sequelae. Abusive situations may occur when a family must provide care or live with an elder family member. Many family caregivers cannot cope with the stress of caring for an elderly parent. Adult children who care for these elderly parents are often dependent on the elder for money and housing (Fester, 1990). They may feel trapped and overwhelmed and abuse their parent physically, emotionally, as well as financially. Negative reactions to elders within the extended family may serve as fertile ground for the negative attitudes towards the elderly in general.

Other individual cognitive and affective factors which may be related to the abusive family include depression (Milner, Charlesworth, Gold, Gold, Friesen, 1984). There appears to be an increased incidence and potential for all forms of child abuse, especially maltreatment and neglect, in parents experiencing depression.

Certain individual personality traits are also cognitive-affective factors that are associated with abusive families. Abusers tend to have higher levels of state and trait anxiety (Aragona, 1983), anger, difficulty with social relationships and less empathy with other people's feelings (Steele, 1987). Abusers tend to experience less enjoyment from family contact (Reid, Taplin, & Lorber, 1981). Spousal battering along with the power and control tactics exercised by perpetrators is a learned behavior and also seems related to personality traits

176

(Joyce, 1993).

The abusive family perpetuates negative cognitive and affective styles in their children. These negative styles can produce depression and other self-destructive behaviors, reduced self-esteem, externality, self-reproach, violent criminal behaviors, dissociative disorders, and a general inability to deal with life stressors in healthy constructive ways (Kiser, Heston, Millsap, & Pruitt, 1991). It appears that dysfunctional, abusive families engender a wide gamut of self-destructive behaviors in individual members. Children from abusive families also learn a whole host of other maladaptive attitudes and unhealthy coping mechanisms to deal with and function in society. Victims of family violence learn many lessons with short and long term implications for behavior.

Social Factors

The family environment is primarily where social skills are first learned by the individual. In the dysfunctional family, healthy social skills are not acquired by the individual family member. As a child develops and moves out of the family environment, this lack of socialization skills may interfere with the formation of other healthy, non-familial relationships. On reaching adulthood, the children from an abusive family may become socially isolated and lonely (Milner & Wimberley, 1980). This social isolation reinforces feelings of worthlessness and diminished self-esteem in these individuals. Relationships with others are dependent on an individual's own self-concept. Therefore, social skills acquired by children through early interaction with significant adults affects the development of social relationships outside the home (Kiser, Heston, Millsap, & Pruitt, 1991). Additionally, when individuals are socially isolated, they tend not to access community or mental health resources. They tend to distrust others (Kiser, Heston, Millsap, & Pruitt, 1991). Social support for the individual is important because it has been found to moderate the effects of stress and enhance self-esteem (Ziller & Stewart-Dowdell, 1991). Social support to a potentially abusive parent also increases the likelihood that the parent will develop healthier parenting skills (Starr, 1988).

In summary, individuals from a dysfunctional, abusive, and/or violent families learn patterns of distrust for others and inherit from their family unit patterns of antisocial and/or self-destructive behaviors that may be manifested over the course of a lifetime. These behaviors, in turn, perpetuate a continuing cycle of dysfunction in the family.

Behavioral Factors

One type of an individual behavioral factor which has an effect on family abuse or violence is substance abuse. Alcohol or drug abuse has been associated with all types of child and spousal abuse. The negative consequences of substance abuse are multidimensional. It creates an environment within the home where substances are used as a mechanism to deal with life stress and events. It endorses these substances as legitimate coping mechanisms and may provide easy access for experimentation by all family members including young children. These substances also perpetuate dysfunctional coping behaviors on the part of the abuser which affects others in the family. In studies of potential child and spousal abusers, alcohol was frequently used by potential perpetrators to control stress (Charles, 1991). Substance abuse has been implicated in all forms of child abuse, maltreatment, and neglect (Milner & Chilamkurti, 1991). Addictions to various substances by a pregnant female can produce developmental disabilities, low birth weight, Fetal Alcohol Syndrome and cocaine addiction in the infant (Stanton, 1990). These outcomes have major implications for the growth and development of children as well as the health and welfare of the family as a whole. Therefore, an individual's dependency or abuse of alcohol or drugs affects their own behavior and may have a negative impact on other family member's welfare and development.

Other individual behavioral factors which must be considered are related to the type of interactions that occur primarily between family members. Individuals within an abusive family are generally characterized by an overall tendency to handle problems in a coercive, physically aggressive manner (Milner & Chilamkurti, 1991). This aggressive, coercive behavior learned in the home can encourage antisocial behavior for individual family members with relationships and activities occurring outside the home.

Summary — Individual Characteristics

The lines separating these four sets of individual characteristics may not be clear-cut. It is obvious that all individual characteristics develop, evolve, and are mediated primarily through the interaction of family members with each other. These characteristics are also altered and moderated by a person's outside personal contacts. Indeed, constructive, healthy relationships outside the family may buffer some of the negative consequences to the individual developing within the abusive or violent family.

There is great opportunity within the violent or abusive family for children to learn many unhealthy response patterns to life events, crises, or stressors. The balance between societal expectations and individual family members needs is not found in the dysfunctional, abusive family. Much psychopathology can be attributed to violence and abuse by families (Kiser, Heston, Millsap, & Pruitt, 1991). Adults and children who are victims of abuse or violence exhibit diminished self-esteem and unhealthy coping patterns and a host of unhealthy behaviors previously discussed.

Motivation - Rewards and Incentives

Surrounding the individual characteristics in the model is the individual's motivational system (see Figure I). In this model, a person's characteristics are examined to determine how they affect and are affected by interaction in the abusive family. The motivational system, why a person desires certain feelings, things, or actions, creates certain needs and produces demands on the family system. The needs and demands spring from individual characteristics. Every person has a specific motivating force for potential needs, demands, and behavior. These are very different from person to person. Needs and demands and the individual's system of motivation may intensify conflict already present in the abusive family. A variety of motivational theories can be used to describe motivating forces. A brief discussion of these follows.

Webster's Dictionary defines a reward as "something given or offered for a special service." Rewards are often categorized as intrinsic (those rewards which produce a sense of accomplishment or internal satisfaction). This set of rewards involves all those intangibles that make a person feel important and enhances his/her self-worth. Extrinsic rewards are those externally provided. These reward systems emanate from motivational theories which help define the value of these rewards to unique, diverse individuals.

These motivational theories can be divided into three basic categories. The first category of motivational theories are "Needs Theories." Included in the first category are Maslow's Hierarchy of Needs. According to Maslow (1970), individuals are motivated to satisfy their physiological needs before they reveal an interest in safety needs and safety must be satisfied before social needs become a motivator. When a need at a lower level in the hierarchy is not met, the individual cannot progress to higher order needs within that hierarchy. Alderfer (1972) compresses Maslow's five category needs system into three categories--existence, relatedness and growth needs. The essential differences between Alderfer and Maslow is that Alderfer does not assume that lower level needs must be met for an individual to aspire to higher order motivators. Because it lacks the rigidity of Maslow's theory, it gives greater insight into the wide diversity one sees with the varying motivational structures for different individuals. The third major "needs" theory of motivation belongs to McClelland (1985). McClelland is less inclined towards a hierarchy of needs but instead examines the specific behavioral consequences of these needs. He outlines three needs. These are needs for, respectively, achievement, affiliation and power. Individuals with a high need in achievement perform challenging tasks well, persons with a high need for affiliation have a driving need to be liked, and, persons with a need for power do well in positions where they can impress or influence others. Therefore, individuals ultimately perform when they are placed in situations that match their specific motivational needs according to McClelland.

The second set of motivational theories are called process theories. Process theories concentrate upon how motivation occurs. The first major type of process theory is expectancy theory. The basic underlying idea behind this theory is that motivation is determined by outcomes individuals expect to occur. In essence, this theory basically proposes that people will engage in those activities they find attractive and can accomplish successfully. The theory also postulates that the attractiveness of various activities depends on the extent to which they lead to favorable personal consequences.

The second major process theory is called the equity theory. This theory proposes that individuals will be motivated if they perceive there is an equitable exchange between themselves and their situation. In other words, patients compare the energy or input they invest in their learning tasks and the outcomes they receive against the inputs and outcomes of some other personally relevant group.

The third major type of motivational theory is an eclectic model which is drawn from needs and process theories as well as the research completed on job satisfaction.

An individual's motivational system in this model is a combination of all these models. The predominating motivational force may be different depending on the situation. Personal characteristics and their motivational system have a major impact on family members and therefore the family as a unit. Motivation has a major impact on all individual behavior.

In the next section of the model, the presentation will focus on the abusive family as a system or unit rather than the individual characteristics of its members. This section has identified sets of individual characteristics that foster various negative consequences of developing and interacting in the abusive family. It also has examined how the motivational systems of individuals may provide can stimulate needs and demands of individual family members.

Family Unit Characteristics

The potential characteristics of individual family members have been discussed as well as individual motivation systems. These are included in the core of this model. The presentation will now focus on the next portion of the model; the family as a whole (see Figure I). To accomplish this, this portion of the model was described using several of the parameters for family assessment proposed by Friedman (1981). The names of these parameters appear in the first circle surrounding the center of the model depicted in Figure 1. They were used because they provide a multidimensional framework for viewing the many aspects of the family as a total entity. These parameters are used to identify the characteristics of the abusive family that appear in the literature on this topic. Although the family is comprised of individual members, the total family is product of their interactions with each other and their environment. The whole is more than the mere sum of its parts. The family unit is critical to the development and health of its members. Therefore, the characteristics of the abusive, dysfunctional, and violent family will be examined as well as the impact of these families on individual development and well being.

Family Traits or Identifying Characteristics

The family identifying characteristics in this component of the model are concerned with data such as social class, social class mobility, developmental history, cultural and religious orientation, family composition, and the family's leisure time activities (Friedman, 1981). In terms of social class status, it has been reported in the literature that lower economic status has a relationship with both child and spousal forms of abuse. It has been suggested that this is because less affluent families may not hide abuse as effectively as their wealthier counterparts (Stanton, 1990). At least on the surface, abuse and/or violence appears to be more prevalent in less affluent families. Perhaps another reason child abuse is reported more frequently in lower socioeconomic groups is that financial pressures so prevalent in recent times and in lower income groups can cause a great deal of parental stress. If one or both of the parents has dysfunctional styles of coping, this may be enhanced by financial pressures. Financial issues can also intensify conflict between spouses. This may result in various forms of child abuse, maltreatment, and neglect.

Family composition may have an impact on family violence as well as on the development of attitudes and behavior of family members. Many of the families in this country are single parent households (Stanton, 1990). This puts tremendous pressure on one parent to meet the wide variety of developing children's physical and psychosocial needs. Since many single parent households are headed by women, it is not surprising that women are the most frequent physical abusers of children (Hawkins, 1986). Birth order within the family may also be a factor in family violence. This is evidenced by the fact that physical violence between older and younger siblings is being reported more frequently (Kiser, Heston, Millsap, & Pruitt, 1991).

Cultural, ethical, and religious orientation are other identifying factors that need to be considered in abusive families. There are cultural determinants of violence. Religious, ethical, and cultural differences between spouses can cause severe disagreement over values and norms of behavior and discipline. This may have an effect on the type and severity of discipline for children within the family (Hawkins, 1986). Cultural and ethnic preferences on a variety of matters may impact on the family's social network and their level of trust for resource persons outside the family's ethnic community. Differences in value structure resulting from ethnic and cultural differences also may cause dissension between spouses in terms of the family's power structure (Joyce, 1993). These values if not in concert with societal expectations, may produce stress within the family. Disparities between family members' values and norms may be intensified by the incongruence with external societal values. The resulting stress may encourage the development of or reinforce dysfunctional behaviors in the abusive or potentially abusive family.

Social Class Mobility of the family as a unit is another identifying factor that assists in the examination of abusive families. If the family as a whole cannot advance socially or economically, there may be increased potential for frustration and stress between family members. Coping mechanisms for handling this frustration and stress by individual members of a dysfunctional family may be limited and erupt in various forms of abuse and violence within their family.

The developmental history of the family, another identifying characteristic, can also be linked to the occurrence of abuse. Families have developmental stages based on various factors including ages of children and related tasks for accomplishment (Friedman, 1981). If these tasks cannot be accomplished or negotiated, the family may develop dysfunctional behaviors. These behaviors may be abusive and can become violent.

Family Environmental Data

There are environmental factors associated with and influence family function that can produce stress. These factors may contribute to and increase the potential for family dysfunction, violence, and abuse. These include the characteristics of the home, characteristics of the neighborhood and the community as well as the family's associations and networks within their community. The characteristics of their shelter can contribute to family stress and dysfunction. For instance, if there is inadequate space within the home for family members or the home environment is unsafe, this can increase family tensions. If the family has little geographic mobility, perhaps they cannot escape the stressors or dangers in their neighborhood. This may enhance the potential for tension within the family and encourage the genesis or continuation of dysfunctional behavior, abuse, and violence between family members as a coping strategy for dealing with these types of stressors.

The family's associations and social networks in the community are an important component of environmental data. Usually, if a family has adequate social support and healthy associations with other members of their neighborhood community, there is a decreased prevalence for violence within the home (Milner & Chilamkurti, 1991). Therefore, the family's demographic or identifying characteristics as well as the family's relationship with the surrounding environment can increase or decrease the potential for negative coping behaviors and resulting family dysfunction, abuse, and violence.

Family Structure

Role assignments within the family are factors associated with family structure which need to be considered in the development of the abusive family as well as the occurrence of family violence. The potential for dysfunction or violence and the actual occurrence of violence can happen when there is role strain or conflict between family members. For instance, there are traditional expectations associated with parent-child relationships. With abused children, perpetrators have unreal expectations of the child in terms of behavior and performance of tasks (Steele, 1989). Parents may also be socially isolated and depend on their children for emotional sustenance rather than providing sustenance to the child. When the child fails to meet the parent's expectations, there is an increased prevalence of abuse (Steele, 1987). An individual family member's role behavior within the family may be predicated on those of previous family role models. Values, feelings and communication techniques are related to these early role models and may color a spouse's perceptions of the other's values and behavior. In the past few decades, the role of women has changed. Many women are employed outside the home. This has required negotiations for change in the role of the husband. He is now expected to share responsibility for child care and maintaining the home. These negotiations can be a great source of conflict and create the potential for domestic violence. These factors also affect preconceptions of appropriate child behavior by adults within the family. Role conflict or strain between dysfunctional family members may have explosive behavioral consequences. Families can exhibit many co-dependent relationships among members with unhealthy consequences. The family as a total unit suffers various negative consequences as do the individuals within that family when this occurs.

The power structures within the family is a factor in family structure and is influenced by individual member's past experience and the perceptions of their early parental role models. The power base of an individual family member can come from many sources. In abusive families, one sees coercive power. Abusive spouses often use physical and emotional abuse to exert power and control over the other spouse. Parental figures use physical or emotional abuse to control the behavior of children within the family. This use of coercive power between family members produces a victim. The negative consequences of being victimized include a diminished self-concept.

Another important consideration associated with family structure is the family's communication patterns and values. In violent or abusive families, communication is poor amongst members. Most abusive families lack cohesion and derive little pleasure from contact with each other (Milner & Chilamkurti, 1991). There also may be incongruence between the value systems of individual family members which, in turn, produces further value conflicts related to other aspects of family structure. These value conflicts can contribute to family unit dysfunction and encourage the eruption of various forms of family abuse and violence.

Family Affective Function

Family affective function is an important factor as to whether or not that family becomes abusive. In the dysfunctional family, there is limited consideration for the physical, emotional and health care needs of other family members. The mutual concern, nurturance, and closeness so necessary for healthy family interaction and the meeting of individual family member's needs is compromised in the dysfunctional, abusive family. Lack of empathy between family members, another affective deficit seen in the abusive family, has developmental consequences for children and certainly has an effect on the stress-related coping behaviors of adults. This lack of empathy and consideration of a child's emotional and physical needs also has serious consequences for their developing self-esteem and self-concept.

Family socialization patterns with the external environment are another set of factors associated with family affective function. This socialization may influence the presence or absence of violence or abuse within the family. It has been discussed previously that parental abuse of children decreases with increased social support (Milner and Chilamkurti, 1991). Social interaction with community members outside the family also increases the likelihood that an at risk or abusive family will seek appropriate resources when stressed. Therefore, the family's ability to socialize with their external environment is important to the presence or absence of dysfunction, abuse, and/or family violence. This external socialization also acts as a buffer for the negative effects of living in the abusive family.

The family's health care function, another family affective function, also deserves mention. Physical or mental illness can contribute to family dysfunction and violence. If the family does not have access to or choose to use available health care resources, physical and mental illnesses that may contribute to abuse or violence among family members may go unchecked. Children who are neglected or maltreated may develop a wide array of physical illnesses and psychological conditions (Stanton, 1990). In abusive families, the health, safety, and welfare of family members is neglected or inadequately supported. Children can learn unhealthy behaviors that persist to adulthood. Additionally, normal growth and development may be altered due to poor health habits. For example, pregnant females who cannot access the health care system or who choose not to participate in pre-natal care may produce low birth weight babies (Miller, Fine, Adams-Taylor, 1989) as well as babies with birth defects.

The family's overall style of coping with stressors is another affective function that is critical to the occurrence of family abuse, dysfunction, or violence. The family's ability to problem-solve, articulate solutions, and implement constructive courses of actions depends on the family's ability to cope with stress/stressful events. Their reactions to stress may include dysfunctional adaptive strategies such as domestic violence. Therefore, events or stressors that tap dysfunctional coping behaviors and exhaust emotional resources of the family are certainly important to the development and evolution of an abusive family.

Summary of Family Characteristics

In this section, factors and characteristics related to the family unit as a whole have been reviewed. In summary, the family as a whole has an impact on the immediate and long-term behavior of individuals within the family. Conversely, individuals within the family have an impact on the evolution of the family unit over time. Since the family influences individuals within the family and vice versa, dysfunctional members may produce dysfunctional families. Dysfunctional families may exhibit many abusive or violent behaviors between individual members.

In the circle outside the family parameters, there are life events or stressors which can potentially impact the family. These will be discussed in the next section (see Figure I).

Life Stress or Life Events

The types of stressors and the life events that create or enhance abusive family tendencies are complex and diverse. The most important fact about these are not the source of the stress or the type of event because these are unique to every family. However, the common denominator regarding these stressors is that they overwhelm the family's collective ability to cope with them. The dysfunctional family is abusive because their collective coping abilities are already inadequate and compromised. Stressors simply produce a further deterioration of these compromised family relationships and individual members' coping behaviors. This may not only result in dysfunction but obviously abuse and violence. Even families who have had normal coping responses can be overwhelmed by a life event and become dysfunctional or abusive if they do not receive adequate resources or intervention. However, in the abusive family, stress and the lack of effective coping strategies enhances further abuse and violence between family members. The effects on individual family members has been discussed.

Consequences of Living in an Abusive Family

In the outer two circles of the model are the short and long-term consequences of life in an abusive family (see Figure I). The total model is situated within society. The abusive family with its short and long-term unhealthy effects on individual behavior, and negative impact on the family unit as a whole, may have equally negative consequences for society. Because the abusive family is dysfunctional and cannot achieve balance between societal expectations and the needs and demands of individual family members, there is always internal disharmony and therefore, some impact on society. If buffers from society can intervene effectively, the short-term consequences of living in the abusive family may be diminished. These buffers are support networks to members or the family as a whole. They offset the negative consequences that dysfunction and abuse has on self-esteem and other individual and family behaviors. The long-term consequences to the family unit and individual members may be modified by effective intervention by an outside resource (Widom, 1989). Short and long-term consequences are included as a component of this model and are modified by buffering forces (see Figure I).

The next step in this model will be to look at short-term outcomes of familial abuse as well as buffers or intervention strategies that may modify negative long-term outcomes. The short-term outcomes will be examined from the perspective of children and adults.

Short-term Consequences — Children

The short-term consequences of family dysfunction and/or violence vary slightly with the type of abuse and severity of that abuse. Children who are physically abused may suffer all types of bodily injuries. Physically abused children are also prone to behavioral extremes. They may be afraid to go home and may frequently run away. These children may exhibit habit disorders, self-injurious behaviors, or psychoneurotic reactions. As with any type of abuse, these children have varying manifestations of low self-esteem. Suicide in children and young adults has been linked to the physical and concurrent emotional abuse children experience in the home environment because it is so damaging to the development of self-esteem (Stanton, 1990).

Dysfunctional behavioral patterns manifested by abused children which includes adolescents may also be evident in the classroom. These behaviors include aggressiveness, hypervigilance, hurting others without seeming to care, and spaciness. Abused children often spill their rage over their mistreatment on "safe" targets, such as classmates and teachers. Many hit when angry and seem to be bullies who pick fights for trivial reasons. Some abused children are terrified of re-experiencing the feeling of utter helplessness and powerlessness, they suffered when being abused. When they fear for their safety or their self-esteem is threatened again, abused children try to replace helplessness with power and become aggressive and lash out in the process. Since abusers are impulsive and lash out unexpectedly, child abuse victims learn to remain constantly "on guard." These children may seem fearful and suspicious and are on the lookout for potential dangers. They are acutely sensitive to mood, tone of voice, facial expressions, and body movements. Children who cannot feel their own pain do not know that others feel pain. They seem cold, hard, and unfeeling. Because these children have numbed themselves to their own misery, they don't even know when they've been hurt. Many abused children dissociate or hypnotize themselves to escape overwhelming thoughts, emotions, and sensations they experience during abuse. In school they become spacey, forgetful, and frequently day dream.

Children who are maltreated and neglected physically or emotionally may also exhibit all the above type behaviors. In addition, they may exhibit conduct disorders related to antisocial or destructive behavior as well as neurotic and psychoneurotic reactions.

Children who are sexually abused may exhibit any of the above reactions and in addition may exhibit promiscuous behavior or sexually aggressive behavior towards other children (See Figure II).

Children's ideas of sexuality are quite different from that of adults, and their attempts to understand sexuality involve distortions and inaccuracies. The disclosure of sexual victimization alters the balance of the family and interferes with previously effective coping abilities. Some authors suggest that children incorporate their parents' reactions to abuse. Children are known to have increased symptomatology, when parents have negative reactions, such as blaming. Symptoms seen in sexually abused children reflect the trauma experience directly, the family environment, the amount of support the child feels, and the level of disruption that follows the disclosure of abuse. Child sexual abuse can be severely traumatizing and emotionally damaging with many long-term consequences for the victim.

Johnson (1991) described a continuum of childhood sexual behaviors with overlapping behavioral consequences. Four different groups have been identified. Group I labeled NATURAL and HEALTHY SEXUAL PLAY describes sexual play as normal information gathering process. Children explore visually and through touch. They touch each others bodies as well as try out gender roles. Children involved in such explorations are of similar age and size, generally both genders, and are friends rather than "siblings" and participate on a voluntary basis. The affect of children in regard to sexually-related behaviors is light-hearted and spontaneous and the children act "silly" and "giggly." The sexual behaviors engaged in may include autostimulation and self-exploration, kissing, hugging, peeking, touching, and/or the exposure of one's genitals to other children, and, perhaps, simulating intercourse. However, these children may feel some shame, fear, or anxiety. GROUP II labeled as SEXUALLY-REACTIVE BEHAVIORS display more sexual behaviors and their focus is out-of-balance in relationship to their peer group's. They describe feelings of shame, guilt, and anxiety about sexuality. Many of these children have been sexually abused. Some have been exposed to explicit sexual materials and some have lived in households where there has been too much overt sexuality. Others have watched excessive amounts of pornographic videos. Parents who have sexually or physically victimized may express their sexual needs and discuss their sexual problems with their children. Children, overstimulated and/or confused may not be able to integrate these experiences and act out the confusion in the form of advanced or more frequent sexual behaviors, and increased interest and/or knowledge beyond age expectations. These behaviors include excessive or public masturbation, overt sexual behaviors with adults, insertion of objects into their own or other's genitals, and talking about sexual acts. GROUP III labeled EXTENSIVE MUTUAL SEXUAL BEHAVIORS have far more pervasive and focused sexual behavior patterns. They participate in a full spectrum of adult sexual behaviors, generally with other children in the same age range, (oral and anal intercourse) and they conspire to keep their sexual behaviors secret. These children use persuasion. However, they do not use force or physical or emotional coercion to gain other children's participation in sexual acts. GROUP III children do not have the light hearted spontaneity of sexually healthy children or the shame and anxiety or the anger and aggression typical of child perpetrators. Sexual interaction is the way this group relates to their peers but expect only abuse and abandonment from adults. GROUP IV labeled MOLESTATION BEHAVIOR involves children 12 years and under who molest other children. Child perpetrators have behavior problems at home and school, few outside interests, and almost no friends. They have been described as lacking problem-solving and coping skills and lack impulse control. They are physically and sexually aggressive and no one describes them as "average children". Their behavior goes beyond developmentally appropriate childhood explorations. Their thoughts and actions are pervaded with sexuality. Their behaviors include but are not limited to oral copulation, vaginal intercourse, anal intercourse and/or forcibly penetrating the vagina or anus of another child with fingers, sticks and/or other objects. These behaviors continue and increase over time and are part of a consistent behavioral pattern. They do not or cannot stop without intensive and specialized treatment. Their behaviors are characterized as impulsive, compulsive, and aggressive, linking sexual acting out with feelings of anger, loneliness, or fear. Coercion is always a factor with these children. They seek children who are easy to fool, bribe, or force into sexual relations. The victim does not get to choose what the sexual behaviors will be nor when they will end. The victim is usually younger by as much as twelve years, since some of these children molest infants. An assessment to use for determining the degree of sexual molestation appears in Figure III.

Children who have been maltreated, neglected or abused in any of the previously discussed ways share feelings of low self esteem and seem to be prone to self-injurious and suicidal behaviors (Kiser, Heston, Millsap, & Pruitt, 1991). Children placed in foster care as a result of different degrees and types of familial abuse may be disruptive and exhibit varied behavioral problems. These children, although removed from the abusive family, may have frequent placement moves when placed in foster care because of resulting disruptive behavior. This may result in a further deterioration to their self-esteem and increased anti-social behaviors (Widom, 1991).

Adults

Besides various degrees of physical injury, battered spouses also suffer from poor self-esteem and in many situations blame themselves for the abuse (Joyce, 1993). They may experience intense anger and hatred for their victimizer (Davenport, 1991). However, they are victims and in essence do not feel free to act. These victims feel violated in inescapable ways and also feel helpless and hopeless. Anger may be the only resource that allows the battered spouse to feel some degree of integrity (Brown, 1978). This anger may be directed towards "safe" targets within the family such as children. It also can have negative consequences for the spouse when interacting with society. To the victim of domestic violence, there seems to be no present-tense method to undo the damage to their lives. Therefore, anger can serve as a protective mechanism against the emotional aspects of the trauma (Davenport, 1991). A battered spouse can exhibit homicidal (Blumberg, 1992) or suicidal behavior. Either outcome is destructive to all family members in the short and long-term. Until the battered spouse/significant other seeks constructive intervention for the problem, they are at risk for self-injurious and/or suicidal behaviors, further physical abuse by the victimizer, and a wide variety of other pathological behavioral consequences.

Elders who live with adult children may experience similar types of victimization as children or battered spouses. Additionally, they may be financially victimized.

Summary Short Term Consequences

In conclusion, one of the short-term consequences of family dysfunction, violence or abuse is the deterioration in self-respect, self-esteem and self-integrity witnessed in the family members who are victims. This deterioration can be manifested by a wide variety of self-destructive behaviors including suicide. The inadequate coping behaviors so often identified in members of an abusive family can produce critical levels of dysfunction and violence. Severe violence or abuse can result in critical or even fatal injuries to family members. The physical injuries that can occur as a short-term consequence of life within an abusive family may also produce physical and emotional disability that persists throughout a life time.

Buffering Mechanisms

The differences between short and long-term consequences of abuse or family dysfunction are not always clear-cut. However, many variables can alter the long-term effects or buffer the negative short-term consequences of life within the abusive family. For this reason buffers modify short and long-term effects in the model (see Figure I). In terms of the model, buffers sit on the line, separating the short and long-term outcomes.

An important consideration in the development of long-term consequences as a result of short-term effects of family dysfunction and violence is the potential buffering effect of influential persons or resources outside the family. Studies which have examined whether or not victims of child abuse always grow up to be child abusers themselves have been completed. Many studies have not substantiated that child victims become adult victimizers as an outcome (Widom, 1989). When previous child abuse victims were studied as adults, it was apparent that many of them had had outside contact with an influential, loving adult that produced some degree of emotional stability. Those adult victims of child abuse who had not been as fortunate did tend to become victimizers of some sort on reaching adulthood even if they were not specifically child abusers (Widom, 1989). Therefore, the presence of a "buffering" adult or influential other with an abused child may be the reason that a child abuse victim, on becoming an adult, doesn't abuse his/her own children. This also illustrates how a buffer can prevent the short-term effects from becoming long-term problems.

If violence or abuse within the family has already occurred, then obviously short-term strategies to prevent or treat physical injury must be paramount. A second critical element in this type of violent situation is to remove the victim and/or the victimizer from the abusive environment

197

immediately and to prevent access to the victim by the victimizer until an effective interventive strategy is implemented. These interventive strategies can be aimed at the victim such as alternative living quarters and counseling. The strategy can also be geared to the victimizer or perpetrator and include removal from the home, arrest, imprisonment, and counseling.

Many different social service agencies and voluntary groups provide services geared to immediate intervention with domestic violence and child abuse. However, the most pressing need is to prevent harm and ensure the safety of the victim.

There is an old adage that an "ounce of prevention is worth a pound of cure." Certainly, interventions aimed at prevention of family dysfunction and violence such as parenting classes need to be a major approach.

In abusive families where the dysfunction does not erupt in physical or overt signs of family abuse, intervention is more difficult. The signs of victimization may be less obvious and overlooked. Therefore, it is imperative that social service personnel, health care workers, clergy, teachers, policemen, and all others who provide services to children and families are familiar with the less obvious signals that there is an abusive home environment. All the resources one can bring to these situations must be tapped. Ongoing exposure, even to a marginally abusive, dysfunctional family may result in a wide array of emotional and psychological sequelae to family members. It is imperative that health professionals become familiar with self-destructive or anti-social behaviors so that intervention as a result of the less obvious abusive, dysfunctional family situations can be accomplished.

Suicide can be a consequence of all types of family abuse. Becoming aware of the signs of imminent suicide is one way society can, for example, provide effective intervention. A teacher who detects low self-esteem or self-destructive behaviors needs to determine if that child is in an emotionally abusive home environment and alert appropriate personnel so they may intervene. That teacher also can provide the type of buffering that may counteract the negative consequences to the child's long-term behavior and relationship with society. Many states have laws which mandate specific professionals to report obvious or suspected physical or sexual child abuse. Therefore, earlier and more effective contact with and intervention by appropriate resources may be forthcoming. What to do in an emotionally abusive situation may be less obvious. Intervening where there are sequelae as a result of emotional abuse must receive equal consideration. In summary, detection of abuse and intervention is one way to buffer the effects of child abuse, maltreatment, and neglect.

In terms of domestic violence, data from the Family Violence Protection Fund survey (MMWR, 1993) determined that few of the hospital emergency departments responding to their survey had policies or protocols addressing the identification and treatment of domestic violence. The number of hospitals with such policies and protocols was well below the Healthy People 2000 objectives regarding this matter (MMWR, 1993). Joint Commission of the Accreditation of Health Care Organizations (JCAHO) in 1992 added an impetus for hospitals to accomplish this objective by mandating that emergency department patient care must be guided by written policies and procedures concerning domestic abuse of elders, spouses, and partners. These protocols and policies are to be added to existing standards of care for child abuse, rape, and sexual molestation (MMWR, 1993).

The recently appointed Surgeon General, Jocelyn Elders, has indicated during numerous speaking engagements that all the negative consequences to children living in an unhealthy family environment occur between infancy to three years of age. More effective monitoring of family life must be accomplished during that time. Programs which assist parents and guardians to meet children's needs during this critical period must be forthcoming. Every dollar spent at this point in a child's life can prevent further, more expensive solutions in place to treat antisocial victimizing adults.

In conclusion, buffering or interventive mechanisms may be able to combat the effects of the short-term consequences of family dysfunction or violence and may prevent negative long-term outcomes. Buffering mechanisms include any strategies that aid in the effective detection and intervention in the abusive situation. Intervention may involve counseling, behavior modification, social support, and a variety of other "buffers." What is critical is that a physically abused victim is provided safe haven and that their diminished self-esteem and self-concept is rescued from further deterioration. Long-term consequences will be discussed next.

Long-term Outcomes of Life in an Abusive Family

The long-term consequences of unchecked family violence or abuse are complex and multifaceted. Prolonged feelings of helplessness and hopelessness as a result of various types of abuse may encourage family members to turn to alcohol or other substances to escape these feelings. The use of alcohol and other substances is devastating to both the abusing individuals and other family members (Charles, 1991). Alcoholism and substance abuse serves to weaken family ties already strained by violence and abuse as well as heighten feelings of hopelessness and helplessness in violence victims. This increases the possibility of suicide and other self-destructive behaviors in these family members. Suicide and self-destructive behaviors are enhanced by substance abuse of any type. Even if prolonged use of these substances is not present, severe single occurrence misuse may be a significant predisposing factor to suicide in depressed young individuals (Charles, 1991)

Children who witness victimization of a parent, as in spousal abuse, have difficulty with their self-concept. Studies show that extreme violence in the family can cause drastic reductions in self-esteem, especially if there is death of a parent as a result of the violence (Ziller & Stewart-Dowdell, 1991). Without proper support or intervention, this long-term deprivation to self-esteem can result in depression, and dissociative personality disorders (Hulsey, 1991). Many child victims of ongoing physical or emotional abuse develop characterological disorders. These include eating disorders as well as schizoid, schizotypal, and paranoid tendencies. Without therapeutic intervention to childhood abuse, specific borderline personality disorders can be manifested at any point in adulthood (Kiser, Heston, Millsap, & Pruitt, 1991).

Other long term consequences of living within an abusive family results in the children of such families having many antisocial behaviors. These may ultimately result in a wide range of criminal behaviors and violent crime on the part of these formerly abused children (Widom. 1991).

The long-term effects of abuse fall into eight distinct categories including social, psychological-emotional, physical, sexual, familial, sense of self, relation to men, and relation to women. Socially, victims seem isolated with inferiority complexes and a distrust of others. Psychologically, victims' reactions include suppression or denial of one's feelings, overwhelming emotions, confusion, feeling dirty, shame, and exhibition of hyperactivity. In females, there is hatred and distrust of men and there may be severe drug and alcohol abuse. Other long-term physical effects of childhood molestation include nausea during sexually connected conversations, gastrointestinal pain with large groups of people, sexual dysfunction, menstrual problems, and feelings of shame for their bodies.

Victims also may become asexual immediately after the end of incestuous relationships and others become homosexual. Long-term effects of sexual abuse include fear of sex, promiscuous actions, difficulty with intimacy, favoring homosexual relationships, and experiencing flashbacks of incest during sexual activity. Many female victims experience abortions and many became homosexual, asexual, or bisexual in their adulthood (Brunngraber, 1986). Effects, consequences of sexual abuse or incest characterized as familial, assume two discrete responses. After detection and intervention, either family members became closer or distant. Some victims became closer to each other (mostly mother and daughter after the parents are separated or divorced). Others suffer irreparable damage to their familial relationships. Their sense of self reflects behavior consistent with a negative self-image, as well as feelings of powerlessness, feeling fat, unlovable, withdrawn and lacking self respect. There were also feelings of persistent worthlessness. Female victims have hostile feelings towards men and are frightened of physical or sexual contact. These female victims also describe feeling emotionally distant from other women, perceiving them as non-supportive and unhelpful.

Lowery (1987) vividly describes the confusions that incest victims endure as they attempt to resolve the persistent memories of their conflicted sexual experiences "I always felt disconnected, somehow not a part of anyone or anything. I always thought of what other people need. I never felt that I needed anything good or that anyone could ever be good to me."

In conclusion, because the child sexual abuse victim has learned not to trust and has had personal security removed, they may feel they have no place to hide, even when they are asleep. Sleeping patterns, especially for women, may be permanently disrupted. A history of abuse may be found at the base of general poor relationships with people, poor marriages, mental illness, depressions, school failure, leaving home, sexual promiscuity, prostitution, and regressive and criminal behavior. Other long-term consequences of family violence, sexual abuse or incest are depicted in Figures IV - VI. These include a flow chart depicting the cycle of sexual abuse and incest that can evolve.

Perhaps, the most devastating long-term consequence of life in the abusive family, is the intergenerational transmission of negative values and norms for family interaction and socialization. Ultimately, this intergenerational transmission of negative values and norms may depend on a variety of factors including the level of family dysfunction, the characteristics of the violence, abuse, or neglect incidents, the nature and severity of the abuse, the age of the child when the abuse occurred, presence of buffers, and the characteristics of the perpetrators (Widom, 1989).

Summary Long-term Consequences

The dysfunctional, abusive family engenders unhealthy patterns of coping in any and all family members. Exposure to these unhealthy, dysfunctional behaviors become part of that individual's repertoire for handling life events and life stresses in the future. Children from the abusive family, on reaching adulthood, carry these dysfunctional patterns of behavior forward to their own family. Even though child victims may not in turn become adult victimizers, they may have other emotional and behavioral problems that plague them their entire life and therefore affect their subsequent partners, spouses, and off-spring. A family that does not have any buffers to offset the short-term effects of life in the dysfunctional family produces individuals with destructive self-concepts who ultimately can produce physical or emotional damage to themselves, others, and society.

Conclusion

In this chapter, the characteristics of individual family members have been examined to determine how these can and do contribute to family dysfunction, abuse, and violence. These same characteristics have been reviewed to highlight the effect of the dysfunctional, abusive family on individual member behaviors.

This chapter also examined the family as a unit to determine how family characteristics can contribute to dysfunction, abuse, and violence within that unit. It also discussed how this dysfunction affects the interpersonal interaction within that family as well as the family's interaction with society.

In the end, the family is the most important asset to healthy individual growth and development. If the family has a healthy exchange between themselves and with society, chances are, so will family members as individuals. Of course, there are exceptions. However, the overwhelming majority of persons living in a dysfunctional, abusive family experience immediate and long-term negative consequences. If the family is dysfunctional, chances are, without outside help or intervention, it will become abusive or violent. In that case, the individuals within the family may manifest many additional destructive behaviors towards themselves, and/or their family, and/or ultimately the society in which they live.

FIGURE 1.1

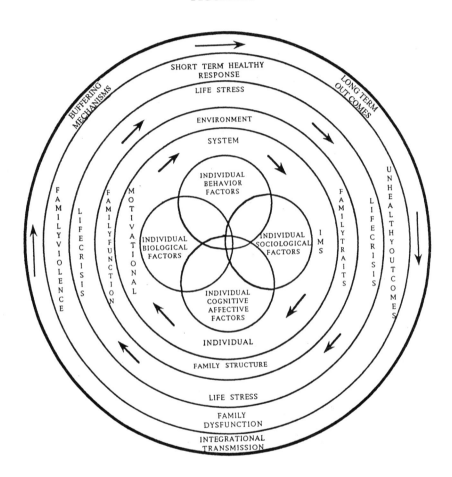

Model developed by M. Stanton, Ph.D., R.N., C. (1993)

FIGURE II

Children's Behaviors
When Children's Sexual Behaviors Raise Concern
Signals for Parents and Counselors

1. The child focuses on sexuality to a greater extent than on other aspects of his or her environment, and/or has more sexual knowledge than similar-aged children with similar backgrounds who live in the same area. A child's sexual interests should be in balance with his or her curiosity about, and exploration of, other aspects of his or her life.

2. The child has an ongoing compulsive interest in sexual, or sexually-related activities, and/or is more interested in engaging in sexual behaviors than in playing with friends, going to school, and doing other developmentally-appropriate activities.

3. The child engages in sexual behaviors with those who are much older or younger. Most school-aged children engage in sexual behaviors with children within a year or so of their age. In general, the wider the age range between children engaging in sexual behaviors, the greater the concern.

4. The child continues to ask unfamiliar children, or children who are uninterested, to engage in sexual activities. Healthy and natural sexual play usually occurs between friends and playmates.

5. The child, or a group of children, bribes or emotionally and/or physically forces another child/children of any age into sexual behaviors.

6. The child exhibits confusion or distorted ideas about the rights of others in regard to sexual behaviors. The child may contend: "She wanted it" or "I can touch him if I want to".

7. The child tries to manipulate children or adults into touching his or her genitals or causes physical harm to his or her own or other's genitals.

8. Other children repeatedly complain about the child's sexual behaviors,

especially when the child has already been spoken to by an adult.

9. The child continues to behave in sexual ways in front of adults who say "no," or the child does not seem to comprehend admonitions to curtail overt sexual behaviors in public places.

10. The child appears anxious, tense, angry, or fearful when sexual topics arise in his or her everyday life.

11. The child manifests a number of disturbing toileting behaviors: he/she plays with or smears feces, urinates outside of the bathroom, uses excessive amounts of toilet behaviors, stuffs toilet bowls to overflow, sniffs or steals underwear.

12. The child's drawings depict genitals as the predominant feature.

13. The child manually stimulates or has oral or genital contact with animals.

14. The child has painful and/or continuous erections or vaginal discharge.

FIGURE III

Assessment

The initial assessment is done to determine where the child may fall on the continuum. It includes:

1. An evaluation of the number and types of sexual behaviors of the child.

2. A history of the child's sexual behaviors.

3. Whether the child engages in sexual activities alone or with others.

4. The motivations for the child's sexual behaviors.

5. Other children's descriptions, responses, and feelings in regard to the child's sexual behavior.

6. The child's emotional, psychological, and social relationship to the other children involved.

7. Whether trickery, bribery, physical or emotional coercion is involved.

8. The affect of the child regarding sexuality.

9. A thorough developmental history of the child, including abuse and out-of-home placements.

10. Access and careful reading of protective services' reports, court reports, and probation documents (if applicable).

11. An assessment of the child's school behaviors when participating in out-of-home activities, such as day care or recreational programs.

12. A history of each family member, the overall family history, and an evaluation of the emotional and sexual climate of the home...

FIGURE IV

Long-term Manifestations of Childhood Abuse

* Sexual dysfunctioning

  - Substance abuse
  - Suicidal behavior
  - Destructive relationships

* Emotional and physical abuse toward children

* Impulsive behavior
  - Eating
  - Spending

* Marital problems

* Difficulty sustaining intimate relationships

* Depression

* Poor self-esteem

* Promiscuity

* Somatic complaints
  - Chronic pain
  - Headaches
  - Nausea

* Feelings of detachment

* Lack of trust

* Feelings of powerlessness

* Needing always to care for others

*   Difficulty with authority figures

*   Inability to deal with incestuous behavior toward children

*   Difficulty in parenting

*   Reinvolvement in incestuous assault

FIGURE V

REINVOLVEMENT IN INCESTUOUS ASSAULT

Victim	Marriage	Husband	Child
Low self-esteem, dependency, guilt, shame, mistrust, history of parentification, sexually dysfunctioning.		Possible low self-esteem. Needs a lot of caring for, dependent.	Birth of child produces marital estrangement. Becomes parentified.
Husband		**Wife & Mother**	**Child**
Turns to parentified child.		Avoidant-continued estrangement.	Incest begins
Mother		**Child**	
Unlikely to recognize what is happening because of our own untreated incest		Incest continues	

FIGURE VI

MANIFESTATIONS OF CHILDHOOD INCEST IN UNTREATED ADULTS.

---

*   Depression

*   Low self-esteem

*   Sexual dysfunction

*   Feelings of powerlessness

*   Lack of trust

*   Compulsive disorders

*   Impulsivity

*   Self-destructive behavior

*   Difficulty in parenting

*   Difficulty in relationships

(Butler, 1978; Finkeliar; Weinberg, 1976)

REFERENCES

Alderfer, C.P. (1969). An empirical test of a new theory of human needs. *Organizational Behavior and Human Performance.* 4, 142-175.

Aragona, J.A. (1983). Physical child abuse: An interaction analysis (Doctoral dissertation, University of South Florida, 1983). *Dissertation Abstracts International,* 44, 1225b.

Blumberg, N. (1992). Battered woman syndrome. *The American Journal of Psychiatry,* 149 (5), 714-15.

Bowen, M. (1976). Family Therapy and Family Group Therapy. In Olson, D. (ed.). *Teaching relationships,* Lake Mills, IA: Graphic Publishing, 219-274.

Brunngraber, L.S. (1986). Father-daughter incest: Immediate and long-term effects of sexual abuse. *Advances in Nursing Science,* 8, 15-35.

Charles, G. (1991). Suicide intervention and prevention among northern native youth. *Journal of Child and Youth Care,* 6 (1), 11-17.

Davenport, D. S. (1991). The functions of anger and forgiveness: Guidelines for psychotherapy with victims. *Psychotherapy,* 28 (1), 140-144.

Fester, C. (1990). Elder abuse on the rise — protection limited. *Christian Science Monitor,* September 27, 1990, p. 12.

Friedman, M.M. (1981). *Family Nursing-Theory in Assessment.* New York: Appleton. Century-Crofts.

Friedrich, W.N., Tyler, J.D., & Clark, J.A. (1985). Personality And psychophysiological variables in abusive, neglectful, and low income control mothers. *Journal of Nervous and Mental Disease,* 170, 577-587.

Hawkins, P. (1986). *Children at risk: My fight against child abuse- A personal history and a public plea.* Bethesda, MD.: Adler & Adler.

Hulsey, T. L. (1991). Trauma and dissociation. *The American Journal of Psychiatry*, 148, 1422.

Johnson, T. C. (1991). Understanding the Sexual Behaviors of Young Children. *SIECUS Report*, 19, 8-15.

Joyce, K. (1993). Challenging the mythology - the truth about battered women. *Haven House Hotline*, Buffalo, New York: Haven House Handout.

Kelley, S. (1993). Parental stress response to sexual abuse and ritualistic abuse of children in Care Centers in Wegner, G. and Alexander, R. 9ed.0 readings in *Family Nursing*. Philadelphia: J.B. Lippincott.

Kiser, L. J., Heston, J., Millsap, P. A., & Pruitt, D. B. (1991). Physical and sexual abuse in childhood: Relationship with post-traumatic stress disorder. *Journal of the American Academy of Child and Adolescent Psychiatry*, 30 (5), 776-83.

Lahey, B.B., Conger, R.D., Atkeson, B.M., & Trieber, F.A. (1984). Parenting behavior and emotional status of physically abusive mothers. *Journal of Consulting and Clinical Psychology*, 52, 1062-1071.

Lowery, M. (1987). Adult survivors of childhood incest. *Journal of Psychosocial Nursing*, 25 (1), 27-31.

Maslow, A.H. (1970). *Motivation and personality* (2nd ed.). New York: Harper and Row.

Massachusetts Medical Society. (1993). Emergency Department Response to Domestic Violence, California, 1992. *Morbidity and Mortality Weekly Report*, vol. 42 (32), p. 617-620.

McClelland, D.C. (1985). *Human motivation*. Glenview, IL: Scott, Foresman.

Miller, C.A., Fine, A., & Adams-Taylor, S. (1989). Child abuse and neglect. *Monitoring Children's Health: Key Indicators*, 2nd Ed., 144-152.

Milner, J. S., Charlesworth, J. R., Gold, R. G., Gold, S. R., & Friesen, M. R. (1988). Convergent validity of the child abuse potential inventory, *Journal of Clinical Psychology*, 44, 281-285.

Milner, J. S., & Chilamkurti, C. (1991). Physical child abuse perpetrator characteristics: A review of the literature, *Journal of Interpersonal Violence*, 6 (3), 345-366.

Milner, J. S., & Wimberley, R. C. (1980). Prediction and explanation of child abuse, *Journal of Clinical Psychology*, 36 ( ), 875-884.

New York State Nurses Association (NYSNA) (1993). News briefs: Domestic violence termed a serious health crisis. Report, 24,(6), p.4.

Pollock, C., & Steele, B. (1972). A therapeutic approach to the parents. In C.H. Kempe & R.E. Helfer (Eds.), *Helping the battered child and his family*, pp. 3-21. Philadelphia: Lippincot.

Reid, J. B., Taplin, P. S., & Lorber, R. (1981). A social interactional approach to the treatment of abuse families. In R.B. Stuart (Ed.), *Violent behavior: Social learning approaches to prediction, management, and treatment* (pp 83-101). New York: Brunner/Mazel.

Sabatino, F. (1992). Call to action against family violence, *Hospitals*, November 5, 1992, p. 30.

Stanton, M., (1993). *Family violence: A model*.: Unpublished manuscript.

Stanton, M. (1990). *Our children are dying: recognizing the dangers and knowing what to do*. Buffalo, NY: Prometheus Books.

Starr, R. H., Jr. (1988). Physical Abuse of Children. In V.B. Van Hasselt, R.L. Morrison, A.S. Bellack, & M. Hersen (Eds.). *Handbook of family violence* (pp. 119-155). New York: Plenum.

Steele, B. F. (1987). Psychodynamic factors in child abuse. In R.E. Helfer & C.H. Kemp (Eds.), *The battered child*, (4th ed., pp. 81-144). Chicago: University of Chicago Press.

Steel, B.F., & Pollack, C.B. (1974). A psychiatric study of parents who abuse infants and small children. In R.E. Helfer & C.H. Kempe (Eds.), *The battered child* (2nd ed., pp. 92-139). Chicago: University of Chicago Press.

Stringer, S. A., & LaGreca, A. M. (1985). Child abuse potential. *Journal of Abnormal Child Psychology*, 13, 217-226.

Widom, C. S. (1989). Child abuse, neglect, and adult behavior: Research design and findings on criminality, violence, and child abuse. *American Journal of Orthopsychiatry*, 59, 355-67.

Widom, C. S. (1989). Child abuse, neglect, and violent criminal behavior. *American Journal of Orthopsychiatry*, 59 (3), 355-367.

Widom, C. S. (1991). The role of placement experiences in mediating the criminal consequences of early childhood victimization. *American Journal of Orthopsychiatry*, 61 (2), 195-209.

Widom, C. S. (1992). *The Cycle of Violence*, Washington D.C.

Ziller, R. C. & Stewart-Dowdell, B. J.   (1991). Life after parental death: Monitoring a child's self-concept before and after family violence. *Death Studies*, 15, 577-586.

PART IV

PREVENTION/INTERVENTION

CHAPTER XII

School — A Significant Part of the Community

According to (Jackson and Prosser, 1989) 'A university education nurtures the creative talent of the youth of the nation. It provides not only an opportunity to develop these talents, but also it teaches the discipline to exploit those talents for the good of the community . . . '

Creativity and discipline are some of the icons of higher education.

Frequently, classroom teaching focuses more on lecturing content than any other teaching strategy, which is a preferable way to convey facts and knowledge; it also provides well for testing -- reproducing content originally presented. This method may also achieve certain social and motivational goals.

Collier (1985) states that in small groups, active learning is more like life after graduation, and is an effective method of teaching for future application. It is difficult to give evidence and to be certain, but the hunch of teachers and students silently may agree on several key points:

M.W. Jackson & M.T. Prosser (1989). Less Lecturing, More Learning. *Studies in Higher Education*, 14 (1), 55-69. (c) (1989). Reprinted by Permission of Carfax Publishing Co, 8 15 81 Massachusetts Ave., Cambridge, MA. 01239, USA.

(1)   that most classroom time is devoted to passive transfer of information,

(2)   that this is a low level of intellectual work,

(3)   that they dislike this low level work,

(4)   that both would prefer to work at higher intellectual levels, and

(5)   that both teachers and students would like students to be more active in the classroom (Collier, 1985).

American higher education will be an even more important institution in this society in future decades as a supplier of more advanced skills as well as a source of greater social equality, continuing social commentary and criticism, and transmission of an ever-broadening cultural heritage, so says Trow (1989).

Higher education is the key institution in American society, source of many of its most important ideas, values, skills, and energies. That will be increasingly true as far as anyone can see.

(Trow, 1989).

As part of The Constructive/Destructive Self course,   a classroom assignment centered on students coming to class on a particular date, prepared to participate in a written assignment for the first ten minutes of class. The question they were asked to think about and later respond to focused on 'Describing programs or planned approaches in the school' each was familiar with toward preventing destructive behavior -- possible self-destructive behavior, even suicide.' Students were permitted to use their home school if they were not originally from the Western New York area. They were also told that their contributions would possibly be part of a literary written project by the teacher as part of a book chapter. They would only be identified as a member of this

---

M. Trow (1989). American Higher Education. *Studies in Education*, 14 (1), 5-20. Reprinted by permission of Carfax Publishing Co., Cambridge, MA.

class group as a contributor. Submission of their written class assignment would indicate permission for the teacher to include their written comments and/or suggestions, at least in part, as was deemed applicable.

Also as part of the class, students were generally actively involved in discussion periods relating to the topic as scheduled, as part of their sharing and learning from each other. They have previously been assigned specific reading chapters in their text and asked to prepare for discussion of life experiences with the class or small groups; at times they discussed audio-visual presentations that related to the course specifically.

From feedback over the years from students as class participants, students have initiated comments over and over again that class involvement and being recognized as individuals gave them feelings of satisfaction.

Comments to follow are examples taken from assignments of 1992; 1993 and Spring, 1994.

Some students identified what they considered as *Causes* of Suicide or *Predisposing Factors* to Suicide, such as,

Pressure to achieve when not capable.
Peer Pressure.
Depression; Hopelessness; Loneliness.
Loss of Relationships.
Unfulfilled and need to succeed.
Worrying about what the future holds for you.
Too fast pace a life, i.e., grows up too fast.
Lack of belief in God.

Breakdown of the family —
    divorce; separation
    lack of set rules or regulations for
      adolescents to follow.
    lack of parental "good example".

Environmental stresses —

people becoming just a "number".
lack of moral ideals.
drug and alcohol abuse.

Self —

insecurity.
lack of belonging.
lack of support network.
boredom with life.
broken romance; rejection.
immature coping skills.

Some students' written suggestions to use the school experiences to encourage a more constructive way of life are as follows:

Provide for more student involvement. Stress peace, patience, tolerance, and cooperation among students.

Develop educational programs, as Self Awareness groups such as Peer group rap sessions, and Self Esteem programs.

Organize Friendship groups for Juniors and Seniors.

Have programs for elementary groups, including first graders.

Organize a Wellness Seminar for all students.

Expect that Teachers will be Role Models.

Provide for improved communication through an Information Center to disburse information in school on -

Friendship Development
Sexual Activities; AIDS;
Womens' Values
Self-Esteem Projects
Pregnancy Awareness
Planned Parenthood
Parenting Programs
Child Abuse
School Hotlines for Crisis; for Suicide

Hotline for Substance Abuse

Arrange for Big Brothers and Big Sisters Programs for underclassmen.

Organize groups into Clubs

Language Club
Sports Group
Focus Group
Anti-Smoking Program - Smoke Free by year 2000!

Develop trial for student offenders using peers for sentencing.

Attempt to include more parent communication with the school.

Arrange for 'Help the Needy Program', example. Provide clothing for those in need.

Have young adults pay back for destructive behavior through community work, rather than expecting parents to pay for their destructiveness.

In his writing on Responsibility, Bennett (1993) described responsible persons as mature people who take charge of themselves and their conduct -- they own their actions, they own up to them -- and answer for them. By practice and example we help to foster a mature sense of responsibility in our children and students the same way we help cultivate other desirable traits, he stated. Homework, extracurricular activities, after-school jobs, volunteer work along with household chores, all contribute to maturation providing parental example and expectations are clear, consistent, and commensurate with the developing powers of the child.

Wm. J. Bennett (1993). Ed. with Commentary. *The Book of Virtues*. New York: Simon & Schuster Publishers. (c) 1993 by William J. Bennett. Reprinted by Permission of Simon & Schuster, Inc.

What follows will be some excerpts directly from students' contributions:

'When people do not fit within the norms or disagree with the norms there may be conflict. There also may be self doubt of feelings of inadequacy. There may also follow thoughts of suicide. Sometimes rigid expectations don't keep people in line or conforming like they are meant to, but rather make people deviate more from the norm. With the awareness in school, like the course we are currently taking, we are gaining insight that throughout our lives may be able to enable us to help others by noticing what they are going through as well as noticing feelings and actions in ourselves.'(Student 1)

'It is the responsibility of the school to provide education on suicide and self-destructive behavior; the school is the perfect setting for information to be passed on to people. School can sometimes be a person's reason for self-destructive behavior or suicide -- pressures, etc. . . but Providing information in schools has the benefits of reaching a large audience and helping students to cope with problems like school that cause this detrimental behavior.'(Student 2)

. . . 'A school can act as a support system for a child and help him/her grow as a child, and prevent a suicide from occurring.'(Student 3)

'The school and community need to listen more often to kids, etc, because these are areas of social learning. They can also be a source of communication when individuals have nowhere else to turn to. The school and community should be more influential in community with individuals because they spend a great deal of time in this system. School not only teaches academic skills, but it also teaches interpersonal skills like for example, ways to cope with stress and it can be influential with watching out for signs of suicide. Because it can educate the public, community also has the power, it too can provide information on disease, coping with stressful situations and prevention to suicide.'(Student 4)

'My recommendation is for the school system to mandate that all children from grades 4-12 participate in a minimum of one hour per week, each school year, in a suicide prevention and wellness assessment class. It should be the same emphasis as gym class, and homeroom period should be used on dealing with serious emotional and family problems that the youth of today are struggling with. Inner-city minority youths should also be allowed the opportunity to attend more than the one hour per week mandated class and be allowed to participate in a voluntary class of the same nature at other times allotted by the school system.'(Student 5)

'The schools should have a place where students can seek help if need be. There should also be short information classes taught in the grade schools to teach younger children how to spot the trouble-signs. Other than that, most of the responsibility should lie within the family.'(Student 6)

'The role of the community is directly related to suicide. Suicide stems deep inside and usually it can be traced to an outside event or a person. It is expected that the environment of community affects the atmosphere and beliefs of the schools and also affect the moods, ideas, and concepts children have about life. The pressures and ideas can turn toxic in heads of students creating a suicidal person.'(Student 7)

'It is my belief that the role of one's school and community can play as big a part in contributing to a person committing suicide as does one's own family life or personal problems. It plays a major role because most people identify themselves around the friends they make at school and the environment that they grow accustomed to (community). If a person does not feel as though they "belong" and are made to feel uncomfortable at school or in their community, it could easily be possible for that person to begin contemplating suicide or have suicidal thoughts. It seemed evident to me in high school those who felt comfortable with who they were and those that seemed to be outcasted by others who thought they were better. Although I believe in having freedom to wear what I want, but students that dress poorly may be judged by people on the basis of dress; therefore, I think a school might have a dress code or some arrangement to make students feel equal. It is my contention that when children are made to feel different (in a bad way) that suicidal ideas can emerge.'(Student 8)

'School and community can provide several roles in suicide and/or destructive behavior. Education is very important for young people who need to be made aware of destructive behaviors or suicidal behaviors. This awareness can help them identify symptoms in peers and possibly themselves. Prevention is primary and support systems need to be available to every student whether they are directly involved or not. Programs designed to promote healthy behaviors and attitudes should exist in every school and community, for example in community centers, mentor programs, and social clinics. As part of the support groups, open rap sessions and counselors should be free and accessible.'(Student 9)

'A desire to learn can give a person incentive to live rather than take one's own life. Interacting with other people in school and in the community can help a person solve her/his problems instead of feeling there is no way out.'(Student 10)

'It is my belief that teachers are great influences for young persons. The positive influence of school and community helps individuals deal with how to live generally. Every individual is different and every life experience is different, and it is possible that school and community can influence suicidal behavior positively or negatively.'(Student 11)

'. . . there is a "breakdown" of values in our society. There are not proper values being taught, and the school and community are much too lax. The main problem is a lack of responsibility on the part of everyone (children and adults). No one will take responsibility for their actions. Everyone is quick to place blame for everything on anyone but themselves. If people were made aware of the consequences of their actions and the repercussions from everything they did, there would be more overall respect for others and themselves. These values of respect and responsibility need to be instilled and perpetuated by communities, and by the schools in the community.'(Student 12)

'. . .there should be more workshops or programs available in community and schools to help young people and adults with building self-esteem, and their worthiness. They need to learn to interact with people in a moral and respectable way (remembering the golden rule). We have taken liberal rights and turned them around to become weapons against our own good will and wellbeing. In school there are mega problems with peer pressure derived from materialistic beliefs, stressing out youth into not feeling accepted or worthy, and many young suicides result. We should focus back on the reality of life and not the materials of life.'(Student 13)

'School courses and activities demand perfection from all involved. Those who are perfectionists will not settle for B's or even a 95% and they cannot cope with mistakes as they strive to be perfect. Also a similar pattern can be seen in the community as employers demand more than their employees are physically or mentally/cognitively capable of producing. People get so wrapped up in sports teams that they feel personally defeated if their team loses. Although divorce has become commonplace, the actual act can be considered a sign of failure. All of these plus many others can be causes for self-destructive behavior or suicide in our society.'(Student 14)

' . . . Schools have narrowed their focus to primarily teaching particular skills, such as reading, writing and computer literacy. Creative and pleasurable pursuits such as art and music, have been discarded with the excuse it is too expensive to maintain these programs. However, it is much too expensive in terms of childrens' futures to not indulge them in creative activities which help to develop a fuller and more appreciative character.

Schools focus on material objects as the goal of adulthood, and emotional expressions are ignored. If a student does not either excel in traditional studies, or desires to explore the world in non-traditional ways not involving going for money and material objects, he/she is discounted as less worthy than their status-seeking peers. Schools need to instill an appreciation for culture, travel, experience, music and humanity. Instilling ethical values is primary in developing students with a conscience.

Communities need to emphasize the kindness of a neighbor or a classical music concert. Schools and communities need to recognize that an individual personality thrives on emotional and aesthetic pleasures rather than monetary expressions of self. Happiness comes from within. Suicide and self-destructive behavior are really outward manifestations of inner turmoil.'(Student 15)

The role of the school and community should be that of 'reaching out' to those in trouble, when students feel they have no one to turn to, or feel there are no solutions to their problem. Every student should be aware that there is help at their disposal.

More education for students, more teachers, and role models would make for valuable resources when students are in need of help. I believe peers and elders have more knowledge about counseling and know how to deal with troubled youth and other people.'(Student 16)

'Some schools are really aware that children and teenagers want to commit suicide and they try to involve themselves as much as possible to help the kids.

There is the social worker, the nurse, the counselor, the teacher, etc., There are also programs that are being developed by the schools to help or prevent teenage suicide.

Some school personnel are under the impression that schools in an affluent neighborhood would not need to be concerned about suicide. This is ironic, since that group seems to be in the most danger of suicide.

Some of the resources available include, Compass House for those who run away from home and Crisis Services, Kid's Helpline by telephone.

If people or the society as a whole were to be a little less judgmental, racist and a lot more understanding and sensitive, maybe our kids would feel more accepted and loved and less pushed to excel (sometimes to extremes) when they are not prepared to handle this stress.

The community may try to do a lot of things to help out, but the fact remains that to cure the disease, the issues must be killed. Nothing will be successful if we leave the infection and cover the wound with a band aid. The healing must start at the very root of the problem. For this, society must go through some fundamental restructuring.'(Student 17)

'I feel there needs to be more education and intervention for children at all levels of their education and learning experiences. YMCA and other organizations in the community have increased programs for improving self-esteem and making children more aware of their values, and encouraging them to express their feelings openly with others. Some colleges have initiated 'peer counselor' groups and other observational programs. I feel they need to be more honest about what is observed in children's behavior, since the earliest possible intervention is the key to an otherwise locked problem or topic.'(Student 18)

'It is a moral obligation that we, the community, concern ourselves and become actively involved with the problems which exist around us. It is my opinion that the schools and community have a responsibility for the provision of mental health services, qualified professionals, such as social workers,

230

counselors, and therapists, within that particular community. Other than the family unit, school is probably the most significant arena where children and youth experience growth and change. In school we learn social skills, how to form and maintain relationships with others, and we develop a sense of self-worth as a result of our academic performance.

Teachers and counselors interact with their students closely frequently and have the opportunity to observe and detect changes in students' behaviors, attitudes and relationships. A teacher who has been adequately educated and has received some crisis intervention training will know which signs to look for in troubled youth, and they can intervene at an early stage of a potentially deadly problem.

Community-churches, social service agencies, law enforcement, hospitals, and neighbors, should all serve as a support system to its' residents. By conducting workshops and seminars to educate families, employers, laymen and others, an early intervention program can be initiated to help persons in crisis. People can communicate and share information in group sessions, and relevant literature can be distributed.'(Student 19)

'Community and school are oftentimes sources of external pressure and anxiety. With change occurring so dramatically in today's society and the prevalence of drug use, a person can become more vulnerable to destructive and impulsive behavior.

Community and school are directly related to suicide. If adequate support systems are not found in the community and school systems, destructive behaviors are perpetuated. People can feel alienated without fulfilling relationships in school or in the community. Alienation leads to lack of self-esteem and self-confidence. Instead of solving a problem that is perhaps temporary, they find a more permanent solution in suicide.'(Student 20)

From the students' descriptions and comments, it is clear that they are aware of multiple problems in the present educational system, even among the more affluent of our society. Their recommendations seem realistic with only general means of attaining the goals they identify, but indicate wholesome thought. Based on these data, personally, it seems to be reasonable to request that all teachers be formally exposed to a Creative Problem-Solving Process Course or class in order to better meet the needs of students who are searching for solutions to their personal problems.

There are many theories and approaches to creative problem solving, referred to as the Creative Process by Davis (1983). He emphasizes The Osborn/Parnes Creative Problem Solving Method, developed in Buffalo, New York, as a remarkable set of five stages that virtually are guaranteed to help solve and find ideas for any type of personal or professional problem. The five stages are *fact-finding, problem-finding, idea-finding, solution-finding,* (evaluation, and *acceptance-finding,* (implementation). The steps guide or tell you what to do at each immediate step to eventually produce one or more creative, workable solutions. A unique feature that each step involves is a *divergent* thinking phase, in which many ideas are generated, then a second *convergent* phase follows in which only the most promising ideas are selected for further exploration (Davis, 1983).

A unique teaching strategy also used in this course with a smaller number of students (when classes were smaller), was Conceptualizing through Use of Fingerpainting. In this particular assignment, students were asked to express their concept of 'Suicide' through use of Fingerpainting, using the basic colors,

---

G.A. Davis (1983). *Creativity Is Forever* (Second Edition). University of Wisconsin. Dubuque, IA: Kendall/Hunt Publishing Company. Copyright 1983, 1986 by Kendall/Hunt Publishing Company. Reprinted by Permission of Kendall/Hunt Publishing Company, Dubuque, IA.

with access to black and white. No additional instruction was given the students.

After the completion, students individually gave verbal interpretations (unrecorded) of their paintings. As an observer of student conceptual illustrations in the fingerpainting format, one can subjectively interpret the motion and intensity of color used, and possibly determine some intended meaning by the illustrator. However, authentic interpretation of this so-called art can only be produced by the individual participant, as to what their intention seemed to be.

REFERENCES

Bennett, W.J. (1993)(Ed. with Commentary). *The Book of Virtues*. New York: Simon and Schuster Publishers.

Collier, K.G. (1985). Teaching methods in higher education: the changing scene with special reference to small group work. *Higher Education Research and Development*, 4, 3-27.

Davis, G.A. (1983). *Creativity Is Forever* (Second Edition), University of Wisconsin. Dubuque, Iowa: Kendal/Hunt Publishing Company.

Jackson, M.W. & Prosser, M.T. (1989). Less Lecturing, More Learning. *Studies in Higher Education*, 14 (1), 55-69.

Trow, M. (1989). American Higher Education. *Studies in Higher Education*, 14 (1), 5-20.

CHAPTER XIII

The Creative Arts

To communicate is a primary need of mankind. The spoken word is not always necessary for the process of communication, rather messages are conveyed through lack of verbalization and via body language.

Primary needs are necessary for survival of the species, while secondary needs may or may not be essential for survival; however, all needs are intertwined and hopefully, each individual will experience secondary needs of love, belonging, status with recognition, and ultimately personal achievement.

Art is the creation of form which provides esthetic experience and rhythm is basic. In an art which uses movement as its substance, rhythm is the basic law. The life of all natural movements is rhythm; Rhythm is pulsation of force in time and in space. Pulsation means that every movement develops organically out of the preceding movement and in its turn gives birth to another, so says Mettler (1980).

She further explains that a movement is characterized by position and

---

Barbara Mettler (1980). *The Nature of Dance as a Creative Art*. Tucson, AZ: Mettler Studios, Inc. Permission Granted by Dodd & McClellan, P.C. (Attorneys at Law) Champaign, IL, on behalf of B. Mettler.

direction in space, and both are relative to the structure of the human body as well as to the earth, to the space that is surrounding and to other bodies within the space. Rhythm involves alteration of activity and rest. So, a movement impulse represents expenditure of a single unit of energy followed by a moment of repose. In the muscles in our body, for example, the pulsing heart relaxes after every contraction. We, as humans, can experience this as a creative need for balance of activity and rest in movement expression.

In all natural body movement is breathing, a central rhythmic coordinator. Realizing that breathing is both voluntary and involuntary, we have the need to approach it carefully and avoid arbitrary patterning. Mettler (1980) explains that all human beings have a need to create, and all should have equal opportunity to express themselves freely in dance. No two people are alike and no two should be expected to move in exactly the same way. Each one of us should explore freely the movement potential of our own body and create unique forms of expression.

Although freedom of expression is the foundation of all truly creative dance, the mature dance artist unites freedom with awareness and control. Continuing on, Mettler states there is no artistic freedom without discipline. In dance, there are two kinds of discipline: outer and inner. The outer discipline demands skill in the execution of movement forms already prescribed, while inner discipline requires the creation of new movement forms which clearly express a definite feeling (Mettler, 1980).

Origin of Music

From Alvin (1966) we learn that some composers today base musical compositions on mathematical combinations, calculated on electronic devices. We have entered a new musical world and man may one day find a therapeutic element, providing that mathematical objective truth can be therapeutic. Electronic music enables man to communicate with a world outside human emotions and symbols.

Early Babylonians and Ancient Greek philosophers related sound to the cosmas through mathematical conception of sound vibrations connected with numbers and astrology. They believed that sound existed as a natural element in the universe but it might not be perceptible to human ears. Man sometimes believed that sound was a cosmic elemental force present from the beginning of the world taking a verbal form. For an example, St. John begins the first chapter of his Gospel with: 'In the beginning was the Word, and the Word was with God, and the Word was God.' (John i,I).

Music, Magic, and Religion

The processes of imitation and repetition are ways through which man learns, develops, and creates. Many of us have observed an infant going through the first steps of exploring and apprehending sound. Organized sound, or music carries meaning and the expression need not be lost completely in mysterious character when it becomes symbolic and expresses a human emotion or thought. When man created music his belief was one of supernatural origin rather than man-made. According to Margaret Mead, some primitive tribes in New Guinea believed that the voice of the spirits can be heard through flutes,

---

Juliette Alvin (1966). *Music Therapy*. N.Y.: Basic Books, Inc. Hutchinson, UK: Stainer & Bell. Copyright (1966). Reprinted by Permission of Rupert Crew Limited, London.

the drum and the bull roarer. This process, when it leads to identification of a human being with a specific sound is of special interest in music therapy (Alvin, 1966).

Music in Healing

There is a relationship established between the person as healer and the patient. The healer using music through the ages has been, a magician - a priest - a physician or a music specialist. So, in any kind of society, Alvin (1966) stated the sick man is attempting to attain cure and relief, and finds himself in the hands of the man who possesses some power over the illness. It may have been based on the willing attitude of the patient to submit to the treatment and on responses to the treatment by the healer. In addition to their musical skill and knowledge, there must be a mutual confidence in the prescribed method of healing (Alvin, 1966).

The Amazing Power of Music

Crowley (1992) wrote about the Neurologist, Oliver Sacks, who discovered the power of rhythm and music in the 1970's, to bring himself down safely from the Norwegian mountain with an injured leg. Prior to the accident, in 1969, Sacks had worked with the catatonic patients, left from the encephalitic epidemic. Most of us remember the 1990 movie "Awakenings," a Hollywood movie based on the 1973 book of the same name. This was the dramatization of re-awakening patients who had been "asleep" for 43 years, generally speaking. Music was utilized along with L-Dopa (drug), and the awakenings were convincing for a time, but they were temporary.

Sacks continues to work with patients having severe memory loss for whatever reason and as an accomplished pianist, he believes music has real value as treatment, and will defend music therapy as an adjunct treatment for many future clients (Crowley, 1992).

Music Therapy and Creative Arts Therapies

Creative arts therapies should not be considered as adjunctive therapies to discredit them as 'real therapies, says Zwerling (1979). Concepts widely acknowledged as important in application of creative arts therapies are,

(1) that the nonverbal media employed by creative arts therapists tap emotional rather than cognitive processes, and they evoke responses more directly and immediately more often than traditional verbal therapies, and

(2) creative arts therapies are based on reality and provide more immediate responses and a real link to the patient's experience rather than something portrayed verbally. As explained further, a problem related to body image verbalized is not the same as a body-image problem lived out in movement. A drawing or stick-figure drawing can convey more about one's home or family than a verbal description.

Those who organize their programs designed to treat people and not necessarily to cure the disease will find creative arts' therapists invaluable (Zwerling, 1979).

Art Therapy and Healing

Art therapists know that the arts are unique in the process of helping people. They can establish a heightened emotional arousal, and, in many ways, they can help the other to learn ways to help him or herself. This sort of feeling and learning enhance the sense of self, and ultimately yield the pleasure that can

Israel Zwerling (1979). The Creative Arts, as Real Therapies. *Hospital and Community Psychiatry.* 30 (12), 841-844. Reprinted by Permission of the American Journal of Psychiatry.

help bind the ego (Irwin, 1988).

Music Power to Heal

The three medical areas that confirmed effective treatment by music therapy are,

1. *Pain, anxiety,* and *depression*;
2. *Mental, emotional,* and *physical handicaps*; and
3. *Neurological disorders.*

Few people actually understand the therapeutic powers of Music better than Deforia Lang, Cleveland Music Therapist. She has profited from singing during her bout with cancer. Although she doesn't believe that music is magic, it can be a potent medicine for all (Mazie, 1992).

Artwork and Depression

Buchalter-Katz (1985), describes experiences with artistic communications with depressed patients in a confined treatment center. She suggested these experiences allow the patients to explore some specifics behind their depression by contrasting reality with fantasy. They also can utilize their strength like ability to follow through, to organize and to complete a project. In some cases there is representation of a happier time or wish fulfillment. They can make decisions related to subject matter, materials and colors used, and they derive some sense of pride which usually is re-enforced by others around

---

E.C. Irwin (1988). Arts Therapy and Healing. *The Arts in Psychotherapy*, 15, 293-296. Reprinted by Permission from Elsevier Science Ltd, The Boulevard, Langford Lane, Kidlington CX5 1GB, UK.

Buchalter-Katz (1985). Observations Concerning the Art Productions of Depressed Patients in a Short-Term Psychiatric Facility. *The Arts of Psychotherapy*, 12, 35-38.

him/her. As observed by the therapist, there is more movement and flow generally in the drawings as patients progress in treatment (Buchalter-Katz) (1985).

Dance - A Creative Art

In her introduction to *Dance* — A Creative Art Experience, H'Doubler (1957) remarked that 'all that man has accomplished has been executed by bodily movement'. And because there is the firm relation between feeling and movement, knowledge of the emotional aspect can be gained by studying movement as a medium of creative experience and expression.

The history of dance, like all arts, follows changes in attitudes feeling and fluctuations in man's concept of art, given to every era in history its distinctive qualities. A dance remains in the visual memory of the observer and in the kinesthetic memory of the dancer. The rhythmical structure of a dance, its design and pattern, can be recorded satisfactorily, which is useful for its creator and for other dancers.

The earliest expressive acts of man were undoubtedly random, probably impulsive movements and unorganized except they followed the natural laws of the functioning body structures. Later in development man acquired a group status and realized a greater achievement than alone. As man came to feel part of a larger unit, his individual desire gave way to group customs. Their dancing began to reflect a wider range of human adventure. Like dancing, his love, fear, hate, and anger, but differently — the dancing became regulated by the

---

M.N. H'Doubler (1940). *Dance, A Creative Art Experience.* Madison, WI: The University of Wisconsin Press. (c) 1940, 1957, 1968. Reprinted by Permission of The University of Wisconsin Press.

D.M. Mazie (1992). Music's Surprising Power to Heal. *Reader's Digest*, 8 174-178. Reprinted by Permission of the Reader's Digest Association, Inc, Pleasantsville, New York.

consciousness of identity with a group.

According to history recorded from the early human societies, dance derived major importance from its function as an integral part of their social and religious life. In fact, religion *was* life which included everything. The bodily movements symbolized all important events in the life cycle of the individual which had both practical and religious significance. A wide variety of dances resulted that may be categorized as three main groups,

(1)   religious dances

(2)   dramatic presentations of love and war, and

(3)   imitative dance devoted to mimicry of animals, forces of
        nature, and of gods.

These three groups were pantomimic and were used to heighten the individual and group states of feeling, as well as initiating magical reasons for the natural processes (H'Doubler,1940,1957).

Dance Therapy

Dance therapy is a psychotherapeutic use of movement as a process which furthers emotional and physical integration of the individual.

Professional training occurs at the graduate level, with undergraduate study training in preparation for graduate study in dance therapy.

The American Dance Therapy Association was founded in 1966; it is located in Columbia, Maryland.

The Association has worked to establish and maintain high standards of professional education and competence in the field of dance (A.D.T.A Brochure).

Dance and Prevention of Stress

Dance may be an activity that contributes to stress prevention, like an inoculation, through cognitive and/or physical action, according to Hanna (1988).

Dance may recount through imagery of kinetic discourse, anticipated events that could be anxiety-provoking have fear of consequences. *Past and current experiences* may also be danced, and it may give an individual a sense of *self-mastery*.

The contribution of dance to physical fitness may counter the negative effects of stress and illness.

Chronic *fatigue* or impact of symptoms of stress, and acute fatigue may be eliminated or lessened by the conditioning from dancing.

The maintenance or restoration of optimal physical fitness can contribute to improved overall quality in later years of an individual's life.

Kinds of Dances Associated with Stress

The categories sometimes blur.

Ritual dance an extraordinary event which involves stylized and repetitive behavior. Dance sometimes is a part of religious expression.

Ethnic dance is *folk* when it is a communal expression; folk dance need not be ethnic, but both can be social, ritual or theatrical.

Social dance has as a key purpose to provide opportunity for people to get together and interact.

Exercise dance includes aerobics, jazzercize, and other forms of bodily exertion incorporating contemporary social dance-like movement patterns with

J.L. Hanna (1988). *Dance and Stress* — Resistance Reduction, and Euphoria. N.Y. AMS Press Inc. Reprinted by Permission of AMS Press, Inc., N.Y. 10003.

musical accompaniment to make the exercises more enjoyable.

Theater dance includes forms of dance that require specialized training that are prepared for onstage presentation and for an audience.

Therapeutic dance activities depend upon the movement skill and vocabulary of the client (Hanna, 1988).

REFERENCES

Alvin, J. (1966). *Music Therapy*. New York: Basic Books, Inc. Publishers.

Buchalter-Katz, S. (1985). Observations Concerning the Art Productions of Depressed Patients In a Short-term Psychiatric Facility. *The Arts of Psychotherapy*. 12, 35-38.

Crowley, Susan L. (1992). The Amazing power of music. *AARP Bulletin*. Washington, D.C., 23 (2).

Hanna, J.L. (1988). *Dance and Stress* — Resistance, Reduction and Euphoria. New York: AMS Press, Inc.

H'Doubler, M.N. (1940). *Dance, A Creative Art Experience*. Madison, Wisc.: The University of Wisconsin Press.

Irwin, E.C. (1988). Arts Therapy and Healing. *The Arts in Psychotherapy*, 15, 293-296.

Mazie, D.M. (1992). Music's Surprising Power to Heal. *Reader's Digest*, 8, 174-178.

Mettler, B. (1980). *The Nature of Dance as a Creative Art Activity*. Tucson, Arizona: Mettler Studios, Inc.

Zwerling, Israel (1979). The Creative Arts, as Real Therapies. *Hospital and Community Psychiatry*, 30 (12), 841-844.

CHAPTER XIV

The Role of Pets in Health and Illness

Karen Allen, Ph.D., Psychology

**Center for the Study of the Biobehavioral Aspects of Health
State University of New York at Buffalo**

In the past two decades considerable attention has been focused on the possible health benefits to humans that may be derived from association with pet animals. Psychologists, nurses, psychiatrists, sociologists, anthropologists, veterinarians, and other researchers have devoted themselves to studying the relationships and bonds between animals and people from a myriad of different perspectives. To date there have been several international conferences focused on human-animal bond studies, as well as an NIH Technology Assessment conference and dozens of additional interdisciplinary meetings. Hundreds of journal articles, book chapters, etc. exist that describe what pets mean in the lives of people, and a scholarly journal called *Anthrozoos* addresses issues concerning the interactions of people, animals, and nature.

Because so much literature about the human-animal bond currently exists, this chapter cannot possibly summarize or evaluate it all. Instead, the central focus here will be to provide a brief overview of the development of inquiry about human-animal relationships, as well as a discussion of empirically-based studies that have considered the role pets may play in health promotion and therapeutic intervention. Individuals interested in a more comprehensive view of this topic are directed to several bibliographies and other references at the end of this chapter. In keeping with the goals of this book, emphasis will be focused on highlighting ways in which pets may enhance the *constructive* side of life as well as diminish *destructive* aspects.

I. Human-Animal Relationships: Why Study Them?

Results of recent surveys indicate that more than half of all American households have a companion animal. In fact, although pets are more common in households with children, there are actually more pets than children in American homes. In a survey of pet owners in 11 states, 87% considered their pets to be members of the family, with 81% reporting that their pets understand feelings of family members (Cain, 1979). Such findings suggest that whatever goes on between pets and their owners, and whatever makes people want to own pets, is worthy of careful study.

In our modern, fast-paced, technologically-focused world, it is not uncommon to go through an entire day with very limited contact with anything *natural*. In a highly mobile society with many people living alone, fewer extended families, increased alienation and fear, and decreased contact with nature, it is not surprising that people turn to pets for companionship, love, safety, and comfort. Although some people say that it is intuitively *obvious* that a bouncing puppy is good for one's spirits or outlook on life, others have been intrigued by the challenge of *documenting* the ways in which pets may influence our lives. Since our culture often considers strong attachment to a pet a sign of maladjustment or a substitute for human emotional bonds, human-animal bond researchers have an especially difficult task. Another problem related to studies focused on human-animal relationships is that often such researchers are perceived to be less than objective in the designs and methodologies they employ. It is not likely, for example, that anyone studying pets will begin with the hypothesis that animals have a *negative* effect on quality of life. Recent research in this area has addressed such concerns and, based upon some of the early case study work described below, has employed increasingly rigorous and empirical standards.

Historical Human-Animal Bond Highlights

Nearly 30 years ago, Dr. Boris Levinson (Levinson, 1965) became the first child psychologist to incorporate the use of companion animals into a formal diagnostic and therapeutic technique. Levinson's many publications document through case studies the role that pets can play in the treatment of young patients. Levinson found that children felt safer and more at ease when their pet dogs were present during therapy sessions. He thought that pets helped to build a bridge between patient and therapist by displaying unconditional acceptance of children and allowing them to feel in control.

Some of the earliest and most influential studies on the effects of pets in a psychiatric hospital were conducted by Samuel and Elizabeth Corson (1970) who provided pet dogs to patients who had not responded to traditional psychotherapy, electroconvulsive therapy, or drug therapy. An intriguing part of this study was that patients and dogs were matched on personalities and nearly all of the patients (47 out of 50) became more communicative and less withdrawn. In this research, however, there was no control group and, for ethical reasons, other treatments had to continue during the pet therapy. Consequently, it is not possible to know the degree of influence to attribute to the dogs, or to some unique *interaction* occurring between different therapies.

After hearing many anecdotes about human animal bonds within prisons, David Lee, a social worker at Lima State Hospital for the Criminally Insane (in Lima, Ohio), decided to test the therapeutic value of companion animals in prison by introducing fish, parakeets, and other small animals as mascots. Lee found that permitting the prisoners (among them individuals convicted of murder, rape and other violent crimes) to care for animals was associated with significantly reduced incidents of fighting as well as suicide attempts. A comparison study was made of two groups of patients, an experimental group with pets and another group without pets. In this investigation the medication level in the experimental group diminished to half that of the control group, and the incidence of violence and suicide attempts diminished significantly as well. (Lee, 1983.) Lee speculates that caring for animals provides an opportunity to express tenderness and affection through gentle touching and caring -- activities that are otherwise largely non-existent in a prison environment. Like the psychiatric hospital study by the Corsons, however, Lee was not able to design a truly empirically-based study, and therefore could not report a definitive cause and effect relationship.

Despite the methodological shortcomings associated with the studies mentioned above, such investigations were the inspiration for other researchers who became intrigued with determining the *mechanisms* by which pets might actually influence our health, both mental and physical. For example, can pets be conceptualized as social supports or buffers to stress? If so, do they provide support similar in function to that provided by human friends and relatives? Or, rather than being a *source* of support, is having a pet a healthy experience because animals provide us with someone to nurture and care for? Can pets be conceptualized as a component of a good quality of life? If so, does such a relationship vary according to a pet owner's gender, level of education, income, age, attachment to the pet etc.? If people with pets are happy and healthy is it because of the influence of pets, or because happy and healthy people are likely to add pets to their lives? Is pet-facilitated therapy a valid therapeutic approach for people who are elderly and alone? These are the types of questions that grew out of early human-animal bond studies and subsequently have been explored. The next section addresses what recent research has demonstrated about various aspects of human-animal interaction.

Disease Prevention and Health Promotion

Although much research has focused on the role pets can play in the treatment and recovery from various physical and psychological illnesses and conditions, studies also exist that have considered how pets fit into a healthy lifestyle and contribute to health promotion. Rosenkoetter (1991) has described a framework for assessing health promotion qualities of pets, from the perspective of how pets may influence life patterns in the home. According to Rosenkoetter, there are several areas especially relevant to this approach. For example, a pet may influence the *roles* of people in a household, that is, children may assume new caring and nurturing responsibilities, and elderly individuals may resume such relationships after children have moved away. *Relationships* are also important to consider because a pet introduces an additional member to an individual's or family's relationships. Pets become part of everyday caring, affection, humor, companionship, and comfort. When a pet dies it is not uncommon for people to feel grief as strongly as would be felt for another loved family member (Quackenbush, 1990). The presence of pets may also positively influence *self-esteem*, because pets provide unconditional and total acceptance, regardless of a person's appearance, age, abilities, etc. Finally, an especially important area that can be used as part of a framework for assessing the health promotion factors of pets is *social support*. From this last perspective, several studies exist that demonstrate the roles pets may play as social supports and social catalysts.

Pets as Social Support

One way in which the buffering effect of social support is hypothesized to work is by actually reducing or eliminating physiological responses to stressful situations. House (1981) suggested that social support may reduce the perception that a situation is stressful, and may also, in some way, tranquilize the neuroendocrine system so that individuals are less reactive to perceived stress. Cohen and Wills (1984) suggested that buffering effects depend upon a relationship between the specific need evoked by a particular stressor and the functions provided by available supporters.

In recent years, several studies and reviews have suggested that pets may provide a supportive function that buffers people from stress and illness (Allen, 1985; Anderson, Hart, & Hart, 1984; Katcher and Beck, 1983). Gage and Anderson (1985) found that among pet owners experiencing high levels of stress, interaction with pets was identified as an important stress management practice. Siegel (1990) investigated physician use patterns among elderly individuals who owned pets and those who did not. Siegel found that pet owners reported fewer contacts with doctors than did people without pets, and also reported that pets, especially dogs, helped their owners in times of stress. In perhaps the most widely cited study about pet ownership and human health (Friedmann, Katcher, Lynch, & Thomas, 1980), a significant relationship was reported between pet ownership and 1-year survival of patients after discharge from a coronary care unit. In this study, pet ownership was found to be more highly associated with survival than were marital status or family contacts.

The correlational data in the studies cited above suggest that pets may function to reduce stress and its health effects by providing companionship, perhaps companionship of a special, nonevaluative type. Beginning with this hypothesis, several studies have focused on physiological reactions of humans when in the presence of pets. Lynch (1985), for example, found that whereas blood pressure rose significantly when pet owners talked to an experimenter, it either did not change or actually decreased when they talked to their pets. Friedmann, Katcher, Lynch and Messent (1983) examined the effect of the presence of a friendly dog on children's blood pressure and heart rate while resting and while reading aloud, and found that the presence of the dog resulted in lower blood pressures both while the children were resting and while they were reading. Others have reported similar findings (Baun, Bergstrom, Langston, & Thoma, 1984; Grossberg & Alf, 1985; Grossberg, Alf, & Vormbrock, 1988; Vormbeck & Grossberg, 1988).

Recent research by Allen, Blascovich, Tomaka, & Kelsey (1991) focused on comparing presence of human friends with that of pet dogs, and examined women's autonomic responses to stress. In this study it was found that, in the presence of their own pet dogs, participants under stress responded with significantly *less* autonomic reactivity (e.g., heart rate, skin conductance response, blood pressure) as compared with being in the presence of their (self-selected) human friends. Unlike many previous investigations of human stress and pets, this study used pets with whom the participants had a self-reported close relationship.

The accompanying bar graphs in Figure 1 illustrate the dramatic differences found between experimental conditions in this study.

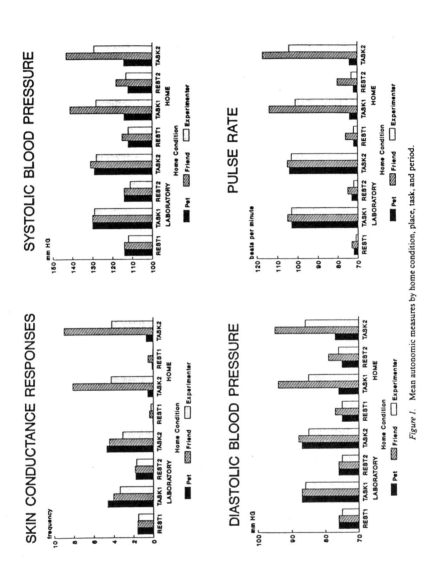

Figure 1. Mean autonomic measures by home condition, place, task, and period.

An interpretation of these findings is that women with their dogs present were apparently less psychologically threatened than were subjects in either of the other conditions (friend present or alone with experimenter). That is, the presence of pet dogs during the performance of a stressful task (mental arithmetic) provided the kind of *nonevaluative* social support that is critical to buffering physiological responses to acute stress. The nature of the relationship between the effects of acute experimentally induced stress and the cumulative effects of the stress of everyday life is not clear (Manuck and Krantz, 1986). However, to the extent that a positive relationship exists, the data in this study are suggestive of health benefits of nonevaluative social support provided by pets.

In another cardiovascular-related study, (Anderson & Reid, 1992) it was found that pet owners had a reduced risk of cardiovascular disease when compared with nonowners. Pet owners had lower systolic blood pressures, plasma cholesterol and triglyceride values. Although pet owners did exercise more frequently than nonowners, they also consumed more meat and "take out" food than nonowners, and the socioeconomic profiles of the groups were very similar.

Pets as Social Catalysts

In addition to acting as buffers to stress for their owners, pets can also fill the role of companions and social catalysts for people who have few other opportunities for social interaction. Robins, Sanders, and Cahill (1991) examined the dynamics of interaction among unacquainted pet owners who met in a park, and found that dogs facilitate interaction among strangers and help establish trust between people newly acquainted.

Pet Ownership Over the Life Cycle

Davis (1991) has considered the relationship between pet ownership and stress over the family life cycle, and suggests several ways in which pets may be used as coping mechanisms. For example, a pet can perform the role of a stress mediator in a passive and/or anthropomorphic manner. In their passive roles, research has demonstrated that talking to or petting a dog is associated with the lowering of blood pressure in humans (Baun et al., 1984; Jenkins, J., 1985; Lynch et al. (1980). In their anthropomorphic roles, pets are considered to have the characteristics necessary to convey love and mutual affiliation.

The significance of having a pet at various times in human development and during life crises and challenges has been the topic of several studies. In a national survey of families (Cain, 1985) the majority of respondents said that their pets were of great importance to them when they were sad, lonely, or depressed, and specifically noted the pet's role during times of crisis such as divorce, illness, and death. In a study about companion animals and conjugal bereavement (Bolin, 1987) it was found that widows without pets who described their health as *good* prior to their spouse's death, reported their health to be *poor* after the spouse's death. For widows with dogs, this was not the case. In another investigation (Gage & Anderson, 1985), pet owners with high stress levels identified interaction with their pets as an important strategy for stress management.

Results of the studies cited above suggest that it is important to study not only the roles of pets in special situations (e.g., nursing homes, children with disabilities, etc.) but also the ways in which interaction with pets may influence our everyday lives. In a series of studies, Kidd and Kidd (1980; 1987; 1989) and Kidd and Feldman (1981); Kidd, Kelley, and Kidd (1983) have demonstrated how human attitudes and relationship with animals may be shaped over a lifetime. For example, Kidd and Kidd (1987) compared the responses of infants to mechanical cats and dogs with their responses to family pet dogs and cats, and reported significantly more attachment behaviors with real animals than with mechanical animals. In interesting studies that examined differential effects of pet presence and pet-bonding on young children (Poresky, 1990; Poresky & Hendrix, 1990), significant positive correlations were noted between childrens' *bonds* with their companion animals and their scores on scales measuring social competency and empathy. These studies adds to growing evidence that *relationships* with pets are more related to favorable outcome than just the *presence* of a pet in one's home. Finally, in other studies by Kidd and Kidd (1985, 1990a, 1990b, 1990c) the focus was on children's and adolescents' feelings about pets, wildlife, and zoos. Such research is important and adds to our overall understanding of the development of constructive and nurturing behaviors as well as destructive and abusive behaviors (directed at both people and animals).

Questions about pet ownership in adulthood and old age have also been the focus of research. Kidd and Kidd (1989) found that childhood experience played an important role in preference and attachment to pets. Adults who had owned pets as children were found to be significantly more attached than those who had not. Since level of attachment and involvement with a pet, as opposed to just *owning* a pet, has been found to be associated with health benefits, such a finding is important for parents considering family pets.

Pets and Elderly People who live in the Community

The importance of pets in the mental and physical health of elderly people has also been a frequent topic of inquiry. Kidd and Feldman (1981) used the Adjective Check List to explore the relationship between experience with pets and personality traits and found that, compared with nonowners, elderly pet owners checked a higher number of favorable adjectives, indicating higher nurturance, independence, and optimism. Because loneliness is often cited as the worst aspect of aging, bonds of friendship between elderly people and pets have also been studied (Peretti, 1990). In Peretti's investigation, which involved interviewing 128 elderly people (64 men and 64 women) in a Chicago park over a period of 10 months, it was found that respondents devoted considerably more time to describing dogs as friends than to describing humans as friends. Perhaps most important and revealing was the fact that 75% of men and 67% of women reported that their dogs were their *only friends*. Further, the participants in this study believed that the friendship bonds they had with their dogs were as strong as their past friendships with other people. The most frequently perceived variables of friendship with dogs were identified by the study participants as:

* *companionship*
* *emotional bond*
* *usefulness*
* *loyalty*
* *no negotiation*

The variable described as "no negotiation" refers to the perception of the elderly respondents that with a dog, as compared to with a human, satisfaction and pleasure were attained in straight-forward interaction devoid of extraneous social dealing or bargaining. For this group, psychologically, their need for attachment was adequately fulfilled by their dogs.

In a study that focused on the role of pet dogs in conversations of elderly adults, Rogers, Hart, and Boltz (1993) found that dogs were a primary focus of conversation, and suggested that pets may serve to buffer and normalize the sense of isolation that often accompanies aging. The issue of access to pets by people who are elderly is an important one to consider, since many apartment complexes, etc. do not allow pets. Studies such as one by Serpell (1991), who demonstrated that pets can provide a buffer that reduces the medical consequences of stress, will hopefully contribute to a greater understanding of the importance of pets in the lives of people who are elderly and often isolated and lonely.

Pets and Elderly People in Nursing Homes

In recent years considerable attention has been focused on pets who either visit or reside in nursing homes. Such programs are known under a variety of names including "Pet therapy", "Pet-assisted therapy", "pet-facilitated therapy", "animal-assisted therapy", etc. It appears that the press cannot resist a story and picture of an elderly woman In a nursing home, complete with an adorable puppy in her lap. The unfortunate aspect of such publicity is that it has raised expectations beyond what should be expected for *any* intervention short of a genuine miracle! Numerous research studies, books, and anecdotal accounts exist that describe the roles pets can play in hospitals and nursing homes, but few such studies are empirically sound. It is very difficult, for example, to design a nursing home-based true research experiment involving such factors as random selection, random assignment, control groups, etc. Ethical and practical considerations make it unlikely that an objective, longitudinal investigation of the use of pets in a nursing home could occur. It is interesting to note, however, that somewhat methodologically flawed research recently has influenced rules, laws, and regulations to allow pets as residents or visitors in most nursing home environments. Several interesting and innovative studies have contributed to such positive changes in legislation, and have focused on trying to demonstrate the many ways in which the presence of pets in nursing homes may be related to positive changes in the attitudes, behavior, and health of elderly residents.

Central to most research about pets as visitors or residents in nursing homes is the idea that animals provide non-judgmental social companionship. Critics of the idea of pets as a true "therapy" maintain that animals are merely entertaining rather than therapeutic, and that *any* change in routine would be just as effective. Supporters of pets as therapeutic agents emphasize that life in a nursing home is extremely isolated and lonely, and that pets provide a type of companionship and unconditional expression of affection not otherwise available. Supporters also say that seeing is believing, and that when most elderly people in nursing homes interact with pets they show positive emotions, and they become talkative and interested in their surroundings. It is hard to imagine that if their were a completely safe *medication* that elicited the responses people exhibit when they are with *pets,* that there would be any question of efficacy. Although this debate continues, currently it is fairly well-established that pets can do much to enhance an institutional environment, for both the residents and the staff.

The results of many studies conducted in nursing homes have demonstrated evidence that animal assisted therapy can be a valuable *adjunct* to other therapies. For example, Fick (1993) found that the presence of a dog positively influenced the goals of a group therapy session by increasing social interactions among residents. Other researchers have examined quality of life issues in nursing homes from both *quantitative* and *qualitative* perspectives and suggest that a combination of these two approaches may be important in understanding how people may benefit from being with animals. Francis (1991) noted that pets were associated with significant improvement on many indicators of quality of life in not only a statistical way, but in ways that can be documented by careful observation and knowledge of individual residents. For example, Francis (1991) found that residents who had not expressed interest in anything or ventured outside for *years* became involved with animals when provided the opportunity to do so.

Pets and Individuals with AIDS or Alzheimer's Disease

One of the most endearing qualities of pets, especially dogs, is that they provide *consistent* companionship, and they are always ready to give and accept affection. This attribute of a pet is very important when a person has a condition such as Alzheimer's Disease. Dogs do not care if you tell them the same story over and over, and they *thrive* on routine, praise, and being petted. Although individuals with Alzheimer's Disease need to be touched and loved as much as anyone else, they often receive less touch from caregivers than do people with other conditions (Beck & Heacock, 1988). Animals can help such people feel loved and wanted when human contact is diminished. In addition, the presence of a pet can make an institutional environment more homelike, and increase the frequency of family visitors.

Since there is no cure for conditions such as Alzheimer's Disease or AIDS, the goal of health care providers is to maintain as high a quality of life as possible, and to address the social and emotional needs of patients. Much of the caregiving for such individuals is provided by nurses, and a significant portion of the current body of research literature focused on pets and terminally ill humans has been done by nurses. For example, Carmack (1991) explored the role of companion animals for people with AIDS, and concluded that animals provide individuals with AIDS with affection, support, nurturance, and acceptance otherwise totally absent in their lives. Participants in Carmack's study were gay men who emphasized that their pets helped them reduce stress, relax, and feel better. Interestingly, pets were identified as an important source of solace, and often, the only one who really "listens," and "the nost important thing in my life." Cormack (1991) notes that adaptive coping to extremely negative life events occurs when an individual perceives that he or she has sufficient resources for coping. Such resources can be instrumental, such as food, shelter, etc., but they can also be emotional, and pets appear to enhance adaptive coping by providing emotional support. The connection between stress and immune functioning (e.g., Kielcolt-Glaser 1992) has been studied widely, and in Cormack's (1991) investigation it is of note that individuals with AIDS consistently described their pets as promoting the ability to relax.

Although human-pet relationships and interactions have been studied by researchers from many different disciplines and from a variety of theoretical perspectives, (e.g., social support, stress and coping, etc.), some of the most intriguing approaches come from the field of nursing. Nurses tend to spend more time with patients than do most other health professionals, and their research reflects their concern with quality of life issues. McMahon (1991) reviewed the literature focused on nursing theories and considered the appropriateness of such theories for studying human-animal interaction. McMahon (1991) noted that a common feature of all nursing models is that they focus on some combination of person, health, environment, and nursing. One of the theoretical models used in nursing research is called Roy's Adaptation Model (1984) which posits that the adaptive ability of an individual is influenced by the presence of environmental stimuli. For example, according to this model, the resources (or stimuli) in a person's environment will be related to the way in which that individual copes with loneliness. Calvert (1989) tested concepts from Roy's Adaptation Model and examined the extent to which interaction with an animal in the environment reduced loneliness in nursing home residents. In this study statistically significant support was found for pets as part of an environment that fosters a state of adequacy by promoting exercise, relaxation, and socialization. Another prominent nursing theory is by Orem (1988) who emphasizes the importance of the role of the family in promoting and maintaining health. Perhaps more than other health professionals, nurses are in the position to observe that for many people a pet *is* the whole family. Acknowledging the significance of a pet to a patient is very important, and nursing research has demonstrated the advantages of regarding a patient's pet as a family member.

Conclusions

In the past twenty years the study of the possible health benefits of human-animal interaction has produced a formidable body of literature. Like any new area of inquiry, human-animal bond research is slowly evolving and testing various empirical approaches. What began as mostly subjective and anecdotal observation has progressed to a stage at which rigorous scientific standards are beginning to be applied. Our understanding of how human health may be influenced by contact with pets will increase if researchers from separate disciplines begin to employ common research methods, variables, etc., and build databases of information. Especially useful would be longitudinal studies that explore the effects pets may have over segments of a person's lifetime. Even from evidence currently available, however, it is possible to conclude that, for people with close attachments and relationships with their pets, clear health benefits are associated with pet ownership.

REFERENCES

Allen, K.M., Blascovich, J., Tomaka, J., and Kelsy, R.M. (1991). Presence of human friends and pet dogs as moderators of autonomic responses to stress in women. *Journal of Personality and Social Psychology, 61, 582-589.* References

Anderson, R.K., Hart, B.L., and Hart, L.A. (1984). *The pet connection: Its influence on our health and quality of life.* South St. Paul, MN: Globe Publishing Co.

Anderson, W.P., Reid, C.M., and Jennings, G.L. (1992). Pet ownership and risk factors for cardiovascular disease. *Medical Journal of Australia, 157,* 298-301.

Baun, M.M., Bergstrom, N., Langston, N.F., and Thoma, L. (1984). Physiological effects of petting dogs: Influence and attachment. In Anderson, R.K., Hart, B.L., and Hart, L.A. (Eds.) *The pet connection: Its influence on our health and quality of life.* South St. Paul, MN: Globe Publishing Co.

Beck, A. and Katcher, A.H. (1983). *Between pets and people: The importance of animal companionship.* New York: G.P. Putnam's Sons.

Bolin, S.E. (1987). Companion animals during conjugal bereavement. *Anthrozoos, 1,* 26-35.

Cain, A.O. (1985). The pet as family member. *Marriage and Family Review,* 3-4, 5-10.

Cain, A.O. (1991). Pets and the family. *Holistic Nursing Practice, 5,* 58-63.

Calvert, M.M. (1989). Human-pet interaction and loneliness: A test of concepts from Roy's Adaptation Model. *Nursing Science Quarterly, 2,* 194-202.

Carmack, B.J. (1991). The role of companion animals for persons with AIDS/HIV. *Holistic Nursing Practice, 5,* 52-57.

Cohen, S., and Wills, T.A. (1984). Stress, social support, and the buffering hypothesis. *Psychological Bulletin, 98*, 310-357.

Corson, S.A. & Corson, E.O. (1975). Pet-facilitated psychotherapy in a hospital setting. *Current Psychiatric Therapies, 15*, 277-286.

Cusack, O. & Smith, E. (1984). Pets and the elderly: The therapeutic bond. N.Y.: Haworth Press.

Davis, J.H. (1991). Pet ownership and stress over the family life cycle. *Holistic Nursing Practice, 5*, 52-57.

Fick, K.M. (1993). The influence of an animal on social interaction of nursing home residents in a group setting. *American Journal of Occupational Therapy, 47*, 529-534.

Francis, G.M. (1991). Here come the puppies: The power of the human-animal bond. *Holistic Nursing Practice, 5*, 38-41.

Friedmann, E., Katcher, A.H., Lynch, J.J., & Thomas, S.A. (1980). Animal companions and one-year survival of patients after discharge from a coronary care unit. *Public Health Reports, 95*, 307-312.

Friedmann, E., Katcher, A.H., Lynch, J.J., & Messent, P.R. (1983). Social interaction and blood pressure. *Journal of Nervous and Mental Diseases, 171*, 461-465.

Gage, M.G. & Anderson, R.K. (1985). Pet ownership, social support, and stress. *Journal of the Delta Society, 2*, 64.

Grossberg, J.M. & Alf, E.F. (1985). Interaction with pet dogs: Effect on human cardiovascular response. *Journal of the Delta Society, 2*, 20-27.

Grossberg, J.M., Alf, E.F., & Vormbrock, J.K. (1988). Does pet dog presence reduce human cardiovascular responses to stress? *Anthrozoos, 2*, 38-44.

House, J. (1981). *Work, stress and social support.* Reading, MA: Addison Wesley.

Jenkins, J.L. (1986). Physiological effects of petting a companion animal. *Psychological Reports, 58*, 21-22.

Kidd, A.H. & Feldmann, B.M. (1981). Pet ownership and self-perceptions of older people. *Psychological Reports, 48*, 867-875.

Kidd, A.H., Kelley, H.T., & Kidd, R.M. (1983). Personality characteristics of horse, turtle, snake, and bird owners. *Psychological Reports, 52*, 719-729.

Kidd, A.H. & Kidd, R.M. (1980). Personality characteristics and preferences in pet ownership. *Psychological Reports, 46*, 939-949.

Kidd, A.H. & Kidd, R.M. (1985). Children's attitudes toward their pets. *Psychological Reports, 57*, 15-31.

Kidd, A.H. & Kidd, R.M. (1987). Reactions of infants and toddlers to live and toy animals. *Psychological Reports, 61*, 455-464.

Kidd, A.H. & Kidd, R.M. (1989). Factors in adults' attitudes toward pets. *Psychological Reports, 65*, 903-910.

Kidd, A.H. & Kidd, R.M. (1990a). Factors in children's attitudes toward pets. *Psychological Reports, 66*, 775-786.

Kidd, A.H. & Kidd, R.M. (1990b). High school students and their pets. *Psychological Reports, 66*, 1391-1394.

Kidd, A.H. & Kidd, R.M. (1990c). Social and environmental influences on children's attitudes toward pets. *Psychological Reports, 67*, 807-818.

Kiecolt-Glaser, J.K. (1992). Psychoneuroimmunology: Can psychological interventions modulate immunity? *Journal of Consulting and Clinical Psychology, 60*, 569-575.

Lee, D.R. (1983). Pet therapy: Helping patients through troubled times. *California Veterinarian, 37*, 24-25.

Levinson, B. (1965). Pet psychotherapy: Use of household pets in the treatment of behavior disorders in childhood. *Psychological Reports, 17*, 695-698.

268

Lynch, J.J. (1985). The language of the heart. New York: Basic Books.

Lynch, J.J., Thomas, S.A., Long, J., Malinow, K.L., Chickadonz, G. & Katcher, A.H. (1980). Human speech and blood pressure. *Journal of Nervous and Mental Disease, 168,* 526-534.

McMahon, S. (1991). The quest for synthesis: human-companion animal relationships and nursing theories. *Holistic Nursing Practice, 5,* 1-5.

Manuck, S.B. & Krantz, D.S. (1986). Psychophysiological reactivity in coronary heart disease and essential hypertension. In K.A. Matthews et al. (Eds.) *Handbook of stress, reactivity, and cardiovascular disease* (pp. 11-34). New York: Wiley.

Orem, D. (1988). The form of nursing science. *Nursing Science Quarterly, 1,* 75-79.

Peretti, P.O. (1990). Elderly-animal friendship bonds. *Social Behavior and Personality, 18,* 151-156.

Poresky, R.H. (1990). The young children's empathy measure: Reliability, validity, and effects of companion animal bonding. *Psychological Reports, 66,* 931-936.

Poresky, R.H. & Hendrix, C. (1990). Differential effects of pet presence and pet-bonding on young children. *Psychological Reports, 67,* 51-54.

Quackenbush, J.E. & Glickman, L. (1984). Helping people adjust to the death of a pet. *Health and Social Work, 9,* 42-48.

Robins, D.M., Sanders, C.R., Cahill, S.E. (1991). Dogs and their people: Pet-facilitated interaction in a public setting. *Journal of Contemporary Ethnography, 20,* 3-25.

Rogers, J., Hart, L.A., & Boltz, R.P. (1993). The role of pet dogs in casual conversation of elderly adults. *Journal of Social Psychology, 133,* 265-267.

Rosenkoetter, M.M. (1991). Health promotion: The influence of pets on life patterns in the home. *Holistic Nursing Practice, 5,* 42-51.

Roy, C. (1984). *Introduction to nursing: An adaptation model.* Englewood Cliffs, N.J.: Prentice Hall.

Serpell, J. (1991). Beneficial effects of pet ownership on some aspects of human health and behaviours. *Journal of the Royal Society of Medicine, 84,* 717-720.

Siegel, J.M. (1990). Stressful life events and use of physician service among the elderly: the moderating role of pet ownership. *Journal of Personality and Social Psychology, 58,* 1081-1086.

Vormbrock, J.K. & Grossberg, J.M. (1988). Cardiovascular effects of human-pet dog interactions. *Journal of Behavioral Medicine, 11,* 509-517.

Research Centers, Demonstration Programs, and Agencies
Focused on Animal-Human Relationships

DELTA SOCIETY - A non-profit professional organization founded in 1977, The Delta Society promotes mutually beneficial contacts with animals and nature.
ADDRESS: Box 1080, Renton, WA. 98057-1080
PHONE: (206) 226-7357
FAX: (206) 235-1076

ANTHROZOOLOGY INSTITUTE - Conducts research about pet-owner relationships and companion animal welfare.
ADDRESS: Department of Biology, University of Southampton, Southampton, SO9 3TU, United Kingdom
PHONE: 0703-594254
FAX: 0703-594269

CAMBRIDGE COMPANION ANIMAL RESEARCH GROUP
ADDRESS: 307 Huntington Road, Department of Clinical Veterinary Medicine, Cambridge University, Cambridge CB3 OJQ, United Kingdom
PHONE: 0223-276225
FAX: 0223-277605

CEN/SHARE - Center for the Study of Human-Animal Relationships and Environment
ADDRESS: Box 197, Mayo Memorial Building, University of Minnesota, 420 Delaware St., SE, Minneapolis, MN 55455

CENTER FOR ANIMALS AND PUBLIC POLICY
ADDRESS: Tufts School of Veterinary Medicine, 200 Westboro Rd., North Grafton, MA 01536
PHONE: (508) 839-5302, ext. 4750
FAX: (508) 839-2953

CENTER FOR ANIMALS IN SOCIETY
ADDRESS: School of Veterinary Medicine, University of California, Davis, CA 95616
PHONE: (916) 752-3602; 752-1800

CENTER FOR APPLIED ETHOLOGY AND HUMAN-ANIMAL INTERACTION
ADDRESS: Veterinary Pathobiology, School of Veterinary Medicine, Purdue University, West Lafayette, IN 47907
PHONE: (317) 494-0854

CENTER FOR THE STUDY OF HUMAN-ANIMAL INTERACTIONS AND SOCIETY
ADDRESS: School of Veterinary Medicine, University of Pennsylvania, Philadelphia, PA 19104

HABIT: Human Animal Bond in Tennessee
ADDRESS: Department of Environmental Practice, College of Veterinary Medicine, P.O. Box 1071, University of Tennessee, Knoxville, TN 37901-1071
PHONE: (615) 974-5633
FAX: (615) 974-8222

IET: INSTITUTE FOR APPLIED ETHOLOGY AND ANIMAL PSYCHOLOGY
ADDRESS: Vorderi Siten 30, 8816 Hirzel, Switzerland
PHONE: 01-729 9227
FAX: 01-729 9286

ISHAR: Institute for the Study of Human-Animal Relationships
ADDRESS: Department of Biology, Leiden University, P.O. Box 9516, 2300 RA Leiden, The Netherlands
PHONE: 0317-1272727
FAX: 0317-1274900

PEOPLE-PET PARTNERSHIP
ADDRESS: College of Veterinary Medicine, Washington State University, Pullman, WA 99164-7010
PHONE: (509) 335-1303

CHAPTER XV

The Use of Humor as a Constructive Life Force

*We are all here for a spell.   Get all the good
laughs you can.   (Will Rogers)*

In the Beginning/In the End: Humor Is a Matter and Life and Death

I first became aware of the positive power of humor in 1977 during one
of the most stressful times of my life. My father discovered that he had an
aneurysm in his aorta, which was a life-threatening situation. My parents and
I flew to Houston, Texas, where Dr. Michael DeBakey was to perform the
necessary surgery. Even though a well-known surgeon was involved, the
outcome was in no way certain. Our family is very close, and the few days
prior to the operation were incredibly stressful for all of us.

Then, the proverbial funny thing happened on the way to the hospital.
My mother and I were staying in a nearby hotel, and each morning we were
shuttled to the hospital by a hotel van driver named Alvin. He had been
selected as Bellman of the Year, and it soon became evident that this was well-
deserved. Alvin had the wonderful ability to invite laughter from people
wrapped in fear and tension as they went to visit relatives and friends who were
hospitalized. His sense of humor helped others to come to their senses... of

274

humor.

It didn't take long for the laughter to melt through the people frozen with fear and tension. People facing grave situations were discovering humor as a beautiful giver of hope and reliever of tension. It created a powerful contagion-- my mother and I, for instance, found ourselves following Robin Williams' notion that "comedy is acting out optimism." After leaving the hotel van (which we dubbed "The Good Humor Truck"), we were in a much better position to help my father laugh off the tension of the upcoming operation. In looking back at that situation, I am convinced that our ability to keep ourselves "in stitches" played a vital part in Dad's successful recovery from surgery.

About a month later, when I was back home in Saratoga Springs, I got to thinking about what a wonderful gift Alvin had given us. He was a Godsend! I then began wondering-- do we have to wait for the Alvins of the world to enter our lives at just the right time-- or could we be more intentional about humor and "make it happen" when we needed it?

I became intrigued with the positive power of humor. Always one to appreciate the serendipity and spontaneity of humor, I began to wonder if it might be possible to invite and apply humor intentionally-- without killing it in the process. Why should such a beautiful gift be left to chance? Couldn't we be more intentional about calling on humor in our lives and the lives of others? I began to explore how we could make sense of humor and then serve it... or more accurately, explore how it could serve us. My purpose was not to "analyze humor to death" but rather to discover practical ways of "bringing humor to life": making humor a life force.

Mythconceptions About Humor

Here in America we have an immensely humorous people in a land of milk and honey and wit, who cherish the ideal of the "sense" of humor and at the same time are highly suspicious of anything that is non-serious. Whatever an American believes about himself, he is absolutely sure he has a sense of humor. (E.B. White)

The above quote captures the essence of the paradox experienced by many people: they value humor personally and yet may question its relevance in dealing with a serious subject like "suicide". This is due to a variety of mythconceptions-- let's take them one at a time:

Mythconception #1: Humor is not serious. We have more important things to deal with than humor.

In fact, there are many reasons why we should be serious about humor-- here is a sampling:

(1) Jest for the health of it! Perhaps the most significant bottom line in life is your health-- without it, you're dead (literally or figuratively). The old adage, "Laughter is the best medicine," appears to be on target. Norman Cousins' best-selling book, *Anatomy of an Illness*, certainly has opened up many people's eyes to the notion that "He who laughs lasts." Cousins, an outstanding leader and great humanitarian, described how he intentionally used various sources (books, films) to tap his own sense of humor, hope, and optimism in recovering from a painful and debilitating illness. William Fry, Jr., M.D., who has done research on the physiology of laughter for over forty years, lends support to Cousins' notion that laughter is like "internal jogging." Laughter can have a positive effect on reducing blood pressure, oxygenating the blood, facilitating digestion, and suppressing stress-related hormones. There may even be a relationship

between laughter and the release of endorphins (the body's powerful natural pain-killers).

(2) In these times, "*stress*" and "*burn-out*" have become household words. They come with the territory of being a human being at the end of the Twentieth Century. Humor can be a powerful antidote to stress-- it can help us to move from a "grim and bear it" mentality to a "grin and share it" orientation.

This notion is captured well by George Burns, who said that "You can't help growing older, but you can help growing old." Father Time is going to keep on marching for all of us-- we can't stop the hands of the clock. But by using humor, we can stop what I call a "hardening of the attitudes." If you stand rigidly in the face of stress, you are much more easily knocked off-balance. If you are flexible mentally, you are in a much better position to "roll with the punches" that life throws you.

This shows up over the long haul, too. In his longitudinal study of what made for "success" in Harvard College graduates, Dr. George Vaillant found humor to be one of the key mature coping mechanisms that insured that stress didn't kill more quickly and commonly. In other words, you can use humor to add years to your life and life to your years. Humor can help us to survive-- and thrive.

Ultimately, stress is not an event-- it's a perception of an event. We may not always be able to control events outside of us, but we can exert control over our perceptions, and therefore, our response to events. Humor can help us reframe stress into opportunities for laughter. One quick and powerful way of doing this is to ask yourself one of the following two questions the next time you find yourself in a stressful situation: (1) How would my favorite comedian see this situation?; (2) What would my favorite comedian do or say if he/she were in my shoes? There is no need to verbalize your response (in fact, sometimes it's a lot safer not to)-- just respond in the quiet and safety of your own mind.

For example, a participant in one of my programs indicated that Rodney Dangerfield was his favorite comedian. He told me that whenever the "stuff was hitting the fan," he would just say to himself one of Rodney's lines: "Look out for #1... and don't step in #2." Another participant in a presentation I made at the Mayo Clinic said that whenever the going got rough, someone would just say the phrase, "Toto, I don't think we're in Kansas anymore," which was a wonderful collective tension-breaker. I've often called on the wisdom of an old sage-- former manager of the New York Yankees, Casey Stengel. Casey was a very successful leader as his string of World Series championships would indicate. When asked his secret, Casey replied tongue-in-cheek, "The secret of managing is to keep the five guys who hate you away from the four... who are undecided."

(3) *"Laughter is the shortest distance between two people,"* according to Victor Borge. This has important implications for anyone in health care, counseling or support roles. Humor can be a powerful-- and delightful-- way to build positive relationships, to increase motivation, and to lift spirits.

Humor is an effective way to create people who are **"inverse paranoids"**-- people who think the world is out to do them good! All the research on self-fulfilling prophecy tells us that this is one of the most powerful personal life tools around. As Phyllis Diller noted, "A smile is a curve that sets everything straight."

Let me give an example of someone who used humor and operated as an inverse paranoid:

This person failed in business in 1831, and was defeated for legislature in 1832. . . had a second failure in business in 1833... suffered a nervous breakdown in 1836. . .was defeated in elections in 1838, 1840, 1843, 1848, 1855, 1856, and 1858. And he was elected President of the United States in 1860.

Abraham Lincoln was well-known for his sense of humor — his inverse paranoia certainly helped him to overcome the obstacles that life tossed in his path.

Metaphorically speaking, it's like the following advertisement I received from Cliff Thomas describing a lost pet:

LOST: Dog, faded brown, three legs, one ear missing, blind left eye, broken tail,   recently neutered. Answers to the name, "Lucky".

Humor can help us to feel "lucky" even in the face of tough times. Humor can help us to feel "connected" with other people. Humor can help us to feel alive... and to stay alive.

Mythconception #2: To be humorous, you have to be a joke-teller. To be humorous, you had to be born with that quality — or you're out of luck (and humor).

I posed this issue to Steve Allen in an interview that appeared in our LAUGHING MATTERS magazine. His perspective is that we may be born with a certain genetic ceiling and floor when it comes to "humor"-- but it's what we do in our lives that influences whether we end up on the ceiling or floor. In other words, there is hope.

Over 600,000 people around the world have now attended our programs on the positive power of humor. About 80% of these people have indicated that they think they have a good sense of humor. Over 98% of them, however, relate that they can't tell a joke to save their lives.

Although joke-telling is one way to transmit humor, it's not the only way. In fact, there are literally thousands of ways to invite smiles and laughter in addition to joke-telling. In our programs and publications, we help people to develop these skills. So, if joke-telling is not your forte, then there are alternatives. Here are some examples to get your mind going:

(1) Put humor into the physical environment — by osmosis, it may filter into individual consciousness. This could be accomplished by having posters with humorous or creative sayings: "The brain is a wonderful organ. It starts the moment you get up in the morning and does not stop until you get to work." (Robert Frost)

(2) Inject humor appropriately when facing a confusing issue or seemingly hopeless dilemma. For example, using one of Woody Allen's quotes might shed lightness and perspective: "More than any other time in history, mankind faces a crossroads. One path leads to despair and utter hopelessness. The other, to total extinction. Let us pray we have the wisdom to choose correctly." Humor can help us to tickle stress before it tackles us.

(3) Anticipate ways of injecting humor into potential conflict situations. This is called "prepared flexibility," which is what life is all about anyway. Having available a repertoire of quotes or phrases may help you through some sticky situations. One popular quote I've seen is, "Save time... see it my way!" Another one used by Renee Kirk is in the form of a sign she pulls out when

appropriate: "Which way did they go? How many of them were there? How fast were they going? I MUST find them....I am their leader!"

(4) Develop your comic vision. Look for humor and it will find you. Make believe you are Allen Funt (the creator of the *CANDID CAMERA* television show) for five minutes each day... especially in the most serious of places. For instance, one of my graduate students recently passed along this sign she saw in front of a church announcing the two services for a particular Sunday: "Theme of 9:30 AM Service: Jesus Walks on Water... Theme of 5:00 Service: Searching for Jesus." Sometimes it seems that you are expected to "walk on water," and yet, you may be searching in the process. Searching for humor is a wonderful way to find yourself and to stay buoyant in life.

(5) Use humor as a tool rather than as a weapon. Laughing with others builds confidence, brings people together, and pokes fun at our common dilemmas. Laughing at others destroys confidence, destroys teamwork, and singles out individuals or groups as the "butt". In the words of one Ohio fifth grade teacher who attended one of my programs: "You don't have to blow out my candle to make yours glow brighter." Humor is laughter made from pain, not pain inflicted by laughter.

(6) Laugh at yourself. It is important that we take seriously our goals, roles, and missions in life... and it is also important that we take ourselves lightly. This is crucial, because there is a cosmic joke being played on all of us. Today, many best-selling books suggest that we should be not only in search of excellence but that we should have a passion for excellence. This is a good message-- that we should strive to meet our individual potential. At the same

time, by definition, human beings are imperfect. So, what do we do with the gap between the perfection we seek and the imperfection we need to live with? Laughing at ourselves is the best way to bridge that gap. We need to be in search of excellence... and we also need to avoid the yoke/joke of perfectionism.

Telling stories on yourself can be one of the simplest, most powerful, and laughter-filled ways to give yourself permission to be imperfect. Sharing these stories when appropriate with colleagues, friends, and family members can also have the fringe benefit of modeling and encouraging others to do the same. It is a wonderful way to take pressure off ourselves individually and collectively.

Here is a true story from Doris Pack, which will serve also as a metaphor:

Some years ago, I ran down to the basement to start up the washer. While down there, I thought to take off my jeans and shirt and throw them in the washer, too. I was standing there in my bra and panties when I heard a masculine voice call out, "Meter man!" I had nowhere to hide. Then I saw my son's football helmet and pennant from our local school. So I donned the helmet, held the pennant, and stood motionless in the corner. The meter man came down and took the reading and turned to leave. I was breathing a sigh of relief until I heard him say, "Lady, I sure hope your team wins!"

You will win if you can develop and use your ability to laugh at yourself. If you've ever been in a painful or difficult situation in which someone says, "Someday we'll laugh at this!"... you might offer the following suggestion: "Why wait?" Laughing at yourself can have both immediate and long-term payoffs. Invest in jest now!

A Final Exam:

OPPORTUNITYISNOWHERE!

How do you read the line above? Some may see it as "opportunity is no where." I would like to suggest that the "opportunity is now here." The opportunity is now here for you to tap the positive power of humor. Laughing matters... it really does! Sense of humor inspires us to keep the faith, keep perspective, and keep on going. Humor is a life force... may the farce be with you!

Dr. Joel Goodman, founder and Director of The HUMOR Project, is a popular speaker, consultant, and workshop leader throughout the U.S. and abroad. His presentations, publications, and media appearances on the positive power of humor and creativity have touched and tickled the lives of millions of people throughout the world. Described as the "first full-time humor educator... in the vanguard of the movement to legitimize laughter," Joel speaks at international, national, and state conferences and conducts in-house training programs for corporations, hospitals, human service agencies, schools, and associations. Author of seven books, hundreds of articles, and several columns, Joel is also Editor of LAUGHING MATTERS magazine. His organization sponsors an annual international conference on THE POSITIVE POWER OF HUMOR & CREATIVITY, operates the HUMOResources mail-order bookstore, and serves as the most comprehensive clearinghouse for people interested in the practical applications of humor. To receive a free humor information packet, send a stamped, self-addressed envelope to: The HUMOR Project, Dept. CK, 110 Spring St., Saratoga Springs, NY 12866 or call 518-587-8770.

CHAPTER XVI

What Does The Future Hold?

Having dealt with theoretical implications and multiple forces that influence suicide in Chapter one, we need to consider a more diverse society for the twenty-first century, and begin to reflect on how the problem of suicide may well affect our society.

There is definitely a need for increased awareness in the society at large, realizing that the self-destructive tendencies in the younger population continue to rise. According to Bennett (1994), suicide is now the second leading cause of death among adolescents, and since 1960, the rate at which teenagers are taking their own lives has more than tripled. He quoted the National Center for Health Statistics for (15 to 19-year olds) in 1960 having a rate of 3.6 suicides per 100,000 population; In 1990, the rate rose to 11.3 suicides per 100,000 population. These figures do not account for many deaths considered accidental and many that are actually due to suicide.

Suicide Redefined

Beauchamp and Perlin (1978) stated two primary reasons for conceptual uncertainty regarding suicide, social attitudes reflected in linguistic definitions adopted by a culture; and, reason for definitional confusion that has to do with different assessments of suicidal *motives*.

Shneidman has suggested that we classify all deaths as natural, accidental, suicidal, and homicidal deaths. In terms of ones own demise, he suggested (1) intentional, (2) subintentional (where the individual has played a partial, latent, covert, or unconscious role in hastening his own death;, or (3) unintentional. (pp. 88-89)

Morality and Rationality of Suicide

There are extremely diverse attitudes toward suicide in different societies. Approval or disapproval of suicide is frequently influenced by ethical and religious considerations. The person who commits suicide is generally not diagnosed as psychotic, but the debate continues about a rational decision to commit suicide; the accountable theory of compulsion, and when the act is considered as voluntary. These are difficult to evaluate. Moral arguments relating to permissibility and impermissibility of suicide have generally revolved around whether or not suicide violates one or more of three obligations: to oneself, to others, and to God. This framework was used by St. Thomas Aquinas and by David Hume.

Based on the principle of community responsibility, the suicide should consider his own interests and all interests of others affected.

T.L. Beauchamp & S. Perlin (Eds.) (1978). *Ethical Issues In Death and Dying.* Englewood Cliffs, N.J.: Prentice-Hall, Inc. Permission granted by Prentice-Hall, Inc., (Div. of Simon & Schuster, Inc.)

The principle of self-determination states the suicidal person has the right to do whatever he wishes with his own life so long as the action does not seriously limit rights of others.

The third principle is a sanctity-of-life principle which would declare suicide as always wrong because nonsacrificial life-taking was always considered wrong. There are many reasons for invoking one or the other of these principles -- they could be utilitarian or theological.

Intervention to Prevention

It seems reasonable if not a moral obligation for a second party to attempt to stop a person from killing himself, realizing there is usually an underlying condition influencing the destructive behavior. It could be a temporary crisis in life, the individual could be under the influence of alcohol or other drugs and almost always the individual is ambivalent about dying -- actually wishes to reduce or eliminate the anxiety rather than wishing to die.

Paternalists and antipaternalists usually agree that it is permissible for someone to intervene where a person seems driven to suicide by a strong compulsion. There are disagreements over cases where the suicidal person is capable of choosing his own course of action, although the individual may be influenced by a terminal illness or a serious depression. Controversy continues over paternalism in suicide intervention. (Beauchamp & Perlin, 1978, pp. 91-92).

G. Menon (1991). *In Social Integration, Age Groups, And Attitudes Toward Euthansia*. New York: Garland Publications. (c) (1991) by Garland Publishing Inc. Reprinted by Permission of Garland Publications.

Euthanasia Considered

The first attempt to legalize Euthanasia in Britan occurred in 1936; In America in 1937 (Nebraska Bill); Efforts in other states were attempted later and legalization has not been accomplished to date in the United States, according to Menon (1991).

Opposition to suicide and acceptance of the sanctity of human life have dominated Western thought since the establishment of Judeo-Christian teaching around 2 A.D.

In 1516 Thomas More wrote *Utopia* in which Euthanasia was first discussed as a humane procedure for alleviation of pain and suffering of the dying. More (1516) in describing Euthanasia, suggested the priest and officials should terminate life of incurables and the suffering (Fye, 1978; Gruman, 1973). Physicians were not actively involved with the dying and the book had little impact if any on the medical profession and society.

During the nineteenth century there were developments in medicine and medical practice which reinforced the notions of contemporary Euthanasia. Public advocacy of Euthanasia began in 1870 in England through the influence of a school teacher and essayist, Samuel D. Williams, Jr., who proposed Euthanasia be provided for terminally ill persons who request it (Russell, 1975).

The advocacy for Euthanasia in the United States began in 1973. By the 1880s some few articles appeared in widely read medical journals in the U.S., followed by debate and discussion, which continue today (Menon, 1991).

C. Everett Koop (1976). *The Right to Live; the Right to Die.* Wheaton, IL: Tyndale House Publishers, Inc. 88-117. Prometheus Books referred to C.E. Koop, January 6, 1995. Permission by C. Everett Koop, M.D.

Euthanasia - A Dilemma

In discussions regarding the right to die, Koop (1989) explained that this is a broad reflection on the moral and ethical problems created by the term *Euthanasia*. He continued, the consideration of the right to die carries with it implications of right of *how to* die. The deliberate killing of one human being by another, regardless of the motivation, is murder. There is some distinction made between a positive, decisive, or death-producing act and permitting death to occur by withholding life-supports or life-extending procedures, and in medical terminology might be referred to as'extraordinary means'.

Technologically, medicine has advanced very quickly, so that understanding of 'ordinary' and extraordinary' care no longer seem applicable. Today, with respirators, pacemakers, kidney dialysis machines, etc., what begins as 'ordinary' care such as the respirator for a patient unable to breathe, may turn out to be 'extraordinary care' in a given case if the patient can't resume normal respirations without the machine. The example given by Dr. Koop is a victim of a car accident from which the patient sustains a severe head injury, which rendered him unable to breathe. If this same patient sustained a spasm of the bladder sphincter, making it impossible for the patient to urinate, he could be placed on a respirator; have a catheter instilled, and be artificially fed via the intravenous method or a stomach tube. With the belief that the patient would recuperate in a few days, the above care would be considered 'ordinary' care. However, with superior knowledge, a short time later, the patient may not be expected to survive without the introduction of the mechanical means, and these procedures would be considered 'extraordinary' care.

The dilemma presented by Euthanasia affect the medical profession but also the laymen. The doctors' malpractice insurance premiums have increased fivefold, and everyone ends up being affected by the extra care and higher costs.

As Dr. Koop explained, the patient's physician must practice defensive medicine, which involves the doctor and the patient.

Sooner or later the patient, or the patient's family along with the doctor will have to face the dilemma of Euthanasia. Once any category of human life is considered fair game in the arena of the right to life, where does it all stop? It could involve a hopeless cripple, a mongoloid, the blind and/or deaf, retarded, and what about the elderly? Abortion-on-demand opens up other abuses of which Euthanasia is number one. Euthanasia opens up opportunity at this early stage of the game for inconceivable fraud and deception.

Koop (1989) explained that decisions made in any circumstance are tailored to the problem at hand, the physician's experience, depth of family understanding, and the relationship of the patient to both. It is almost impossible to have a set of rules to govern this circumstance; perhaps guidelines but not rules. He believes that theological principles, possibly vague from early religious training, are probably at work in the minds of most physicians as they face some of these life and death decisions. If there is not to be a Judeo-Christian Ethic in the preservation of life in those matters relating to Euthanasia, what does the future hold? (Koop, 1989)

The Aging Society Reaches Out

In the 90s in our present society, most adults know the name Kevorkian, and the majority would associate the name with the M.D. who has created a real question about the right that individuals with terminal illnesses have to be relieved of their suffering by their own intervention. This same doctor provides personal counsel for certain individuals who seek his assistance in the dying process. Although the inference has been made earlier that there are differences of opinion and personal convictions regarding the right of taking one's own life, doctors who have been educated in the field of medicine and have attained their Doctorate in Medicine (MD) in the past, have taken the Hippocratic Oath that bound them to life orientation with no option to assist directly in the dying process.

One recent article (locally) was entitled: 'Euthanasia in the pre-Kevorkian era', (Requiem for the Hemlock Quarterly), that explained the Hemlock Society's newsletter as the true cradle of the right-to-die revolution. The Hemlock title comes from any of the poisonous herbs of the carrot family; a poisonous drink is made from the fruit of the hemlock, according to Webster's Dictionary.

The author explained that the Hemlock Quarterly was an unassuming little newspaper and until recently was the chief prerequisite of membership in the Hemlock Society. Fadsman, (1994), believes this may have been the only radical publication in the United States whose subscriber rolls were dominated by affluent white women with gray hair. Her personal description was, these women probably were the sort of community-minded grandmothers who never littered, never stole anyone's parking spot, and probably always returned library books on time.

In reference to the Hemlock Quarterly, it was published from 1980 to 1993, at which time it was replaced by a bimonthly called Time Lines to publish more diverse material.

When the First Voluntary Conference of The Hemlock Society was held in San Francisco, in 1983, in a Unitarian church, this was pre-Kevorkian and the right-to-die movement was still young and pure. Most of the presentations at the conference referred to passive Euthanasia, or letting people die: hospices, living wills, and pulling plugs. The Hemlock Quarterly, however, advocated active Euthanasia, or helping people die.

The Hemlock Society was launched in Los Angeles in the summer of 1980 by a British Journalist, Derek Humphrey. If any matter concerning Euthanasia appeared in The New York Times (front page) one could be certain it had been reported years earlier by The Hemlock Quarterly.

Some of the content was sharing of cheerful stories about family members making their exits, and the HQ eventually became a how-to magazine. In the beginning vague references were printed for fear of prosecution. Then a few books on Toxicology and Pharmacological Basis of Therapeutics were made available at the library (Fadiman, 1994).

There has been a rapid shift in public opinion regarding suicide in the last decade, and the shift is largely ascribed to the Hemlock Society's 1991 publication, 'Final Exit' Manual that became a best-seller.

These data are part of history and they seem to serve as examples of changing lifestyle, described by Burman in Chapter four, who explained that the acquired bad habits in the twentieth century, from whatever influence, radically inverted common American standards of personal conduct. Moral righteousness went out of style, so to speak, with little restraint on bad habits.

The reader has the responsibility to question and attempt to interpret behaviors of generations past and present to better understand overt and subtle influences on society, from what they see, what they hear, what they read, and what they *feel*.

A. Fadiman (4 Sept., 1994). Requiem for the Hemlock Quarterly. *Buffalo Magazine of the Buffalo News*. Reprinted by Permission of *The Buffalo News*.

REFERENCES

Baird, R.M. and Rosenbaum, S.E. (Eds.) (1989). Buffalo: Prometheus Books.

Beauchamp, T.L. and Perlin, S.(Eds.) (1978). *Ethical Issues In Death and Dying.* Englewood Cliffs, N.J.: Prentice-Hall Inc.

Bennett, W.J. (1994). *The Index of Leading Cultural Indicators.* New York: Simon and Schuster (A Touchstone Book).

Fadiman, A. (4 Sept, 1994). Requiem for the Hemlock Quarterly *Buffalo — Magaine of The Buffalo News.*

Koop, C. Everett. (1076) *The Right to Live; The Right to Die.* Wheaton, Illinois: Tyndale House Publishers, Inc., pp. 88-117.

Menon, G. (1991). *In Social Integration, Age Groups, And Attitudes Towards Euthanasia.* New York: Garland Publications.

SUGGESTED REFERENCES

Bennett, W.J. (Ed. with Commentary) (1993). *The Book of Virtues.* New York: Simon and Schuster.

Jacobs, S. (1993). *Pathologic Grief - Maladaptation to Loss.* Washington, D.C.: American Psychiatric Press, Inc.

Kohl, M.,(Ed.) (1975). *Beneficient Euthanasia.* Buffalo, New York: Prometheus Books.

Thomasma, D.C. and Graber, G.C. (1990). *EUTHANASIA - Toward An Ethical Social Policy.* New York: Continuum Publishing Company.

INDEX

STUDIES IN HEALTH AND HUMAN SERVICES